AMERICA'S LITERACY CHAMPION

Life's Playbook For Success
Secrets from the Verizon Academic All-America® Hall of Famers

3rd Edition

Contents

verizon

AMERICA'S LITERACY CHAMPION

Verizon
READS
AMERICA'S LITERACY CHAMPION

To learn more about Verizon's work with local and national literacy initiatives,
visit Verizon Literacy Network at **verizonreads.net**. Life's Playbook is
also available online, with information on the Verizon Academic All-America
Hall of Famers, information on careers and résumés, fun quizzes, activities
and more! Plus, check out Click, an interactive online miniseries
based on the themes of the Life's Playbook Program. You'll find
Life's Playbook and Click at **verizonreads.net/lifesplaybook**.

*Life's Playbook For Success was recognized with
a 1999 Distinguished Achievement Award by the Educational Press Association of America.*

Additional copies of this book may be ordered for $10 per copy.
Discounts are available for multiple copies.
To place an order or for more information, please call 800-315-5010.

Foreword

Verizon has long believed that the ability to read, write and communicate is the foundation for success in life. It is key to individual freedom and, as such, is critical to America's democracy and free enterprise system.

For 40 million Americans with very low literacy skills, it is a struggle to read to their children. They cannot understand instructions on an appliance warranty or find an intersection on a street map. Equally disturbing are that facts that 43 percent of those with the lowest literacy skills live in poverty and nearly one-third of prison inmates have very low literacy skills.

That is why Verizon has been singularly committed to boosting literacy levels in America for the better part of a decade. Our company supports adult, child and family literacy nationwide through a number of literacy initiatives.

And so, it is with tremendous pride and pleasure that Verizon Communications presents Life's Playbook for Success. This publication will introduce you to some people who could very possibly change the way you view success in life.

I believe that each of us possesses the ability to achieve greatness in our lives. I also believe that each of us can learn a great deal from individuals who have distinguished themselves through their accomplishments and character.

The ability to inspire is precisely what the individuals named to the Verizon Academic All-America Hall of Fame are all about. The men and women featured in this book will likely inspire you to achieve excellence in your own life, now and in the future.

With that in mind, in addition to topics like perseverance, teamwork and mentors, you'll find invaluable information in this book — in the words of the Hall of Famers themselves — on the crucial importance of reading, and of tackling America's literacy challenges together.

It is our honor to bring the Verizon Academic All-America Hall of Famers to you in the absorbing and enlightening pages that follow.

Charles R. Lee

Charles R. Lee
Chairman and
Co-Chief Executive Officer,
Verizon Communications

This is an exciting book.

Not because I've been given the honor of writing the introduction. And not just because it celebrates a truly elite class of American hero. But because this book is a blueprint for success for any student, young or old. The stories and quotes on the pages that follow provide insights and tips that can help shape your outlook and direction in life. And who among us couldn't use a little of that? That's just one of the reasons I'm grateful to Verizon for allowing me to be a part of the worthwhile effort! • In *Life's Playbook for Success*, you'll come face to face with men and women who have received one of the highest honors scholar-athletes in our country can achieve: membership in the Verizon Academic All-America Hall of Fame. • What these Hall of Famers have to say about success goes well beyond sports. You'll find their thoughts wide-ranging. Their anecdotes, without

exception, fascinating in their humanity. The topics they choose to focus on are sometimes surprising. • You'll identify with some more than others. You'll take some of their advice to heart, and no doubt discard some. You'll agree with some of their thoughts, perhaps disagree with others. And if you look closely, you'll see your own life, in all its potential, mirrored — and foreshadowed — in their trials and their accomplishments. • The saddest thing that can happen in a life, I feel, is to "under-dream." If you take away one piece of wisdom after reading *Life's Playbook for Success*, I hope it will be that. You'll find that the Hall of Famers have learned how to dream. They've also learned how to clear life's hurdles and win. So can you. And that alone is reason to sit up and listen. • Particularly noteworthy are the Hall of Famers' comments on the subject of reading. The challenge of low literacy in our society is a daunting one. It's a problem that many keep hidden, out of shame and embarrassment. The words of wisdom herein on the subject of literacy are ones that, as a supporter of

Verizon's role as America's literacy champion, I hope you'll take particularly to heart. • When I think of the Verizon Academic All-America Teams, I think of the ancient Greek ethic of "a sound mind and a sound body." A cliché? Certainly. But to me, that's still the guiding principle of excellence in any culture, and the Hall of Famers on the following pages embody that ethic to the bone. By following their example, in my opinion, you just can't miss. • But wait. How were these men and women selected as Hall of Famers? Just who are they? The Verizon Academic All-America Hall of Fame members were named during their college years to the Verizon Academic All-America Teams. The Teams Program annually honors almost 700 college and university student-athletes on five men's teams (football, basketball, baseball, softball, fall/winter at-large and spring at-large) and five women's teams (volleyball, basketball, softball, fall/winter at-large and spring at-large). Many college Academic All-America

Nearly 700 students are named to the Verizon Academic All-America Teams each year. To the right are just a few recent Team members. ➤ ➤ ➤ ➤ ➤

winners have gone on to national championship teams. Others have been named national players of the year in their sport. But only those Team members who have made outstanding accomplishments in their profession, and made similarly substantial contributions to their community, are nominated to the Hall of Fame. And only the best among those are admitted. • One final note. When I was in college, I desperately wanted to qualify for the Academic All-America Teams — and couldn't. I had the marks on the academic side, but just didn't have what it took in athletics. Looking back on my sports-commentating career, I joke that I always talked a better game than I played. The point is that I had a dream. Perhaps I didn't rise to breathe the rarefied air that the superstars in this book did, but my dream took me where I am today. Yours can do the same for you.
Dick Enberg

Amy Acuff
U. of California-L.A.

Rebecca Lobo
U. of Connecticut

Peyton Manning
U. of Tennessee-
Knoxville

Tiki Barber
U. of Virginia

Adonal Foyle
Colgate

◄ **Dick Enberg** is one of the premier hosts and play-by-play announcers in sports broadcasting, on the scene at virtually every major sporting event, including the Olympics, the Super Bowl, the World Series, Wimbledon, U.S. Open Golf and the Breeders Cup. He has won eleven Emmy Awards for broadcasting, production and writing and is one of only four sportscasters honored with a star on the Hollywood Walk of Fame. In addition to his duties with CBS Sports, he is the spokesperson for the Verizon Academic All-America (AAA) Teams program and host of the Verizon AAA Hall of Fame.

persistence

fear

character

hardwork

humility

ambition

advice

winning

reward

rules

focus

failure

Life's Playbook For Success
Essays and Quotes

HALL OF FAMER

Expectations and Realities

"That's not the way life is."

STATS

- Political science major who graduated with honors from the University of Florida in 1972.

- 1969 All-American football player for the Gators, he set all the receiving records, including season records for receptions, yards and touchdowns — with the first two still standing.

- Graduated with honors, Duke University Law School.

- Currently practicing law in the area of environmental and land use litigation; Chairman of the Florida Elections Commission.

- Active in the Cuban community and a recipient of the Key to the City for Outstanding Achievement in both Miami and Tampa.

You might say I was at the height of my career when it happened.

I had made All-American in football as a college sophomore, which was very unusual at the time. I had set all the existing Southeastern Conference records, some of which are still standing today. Talk about being on top of the world.

Then, one day during my junior year, doing some training, I was out on the running track and out of nowhere my knee swelled up — just out of the blue. I hadn't done anything to injure it, that I could remember anyway. It was unbelievably painful, and I could barely walk.

It was the beginning of a long journey, in which one orthopedic surgeon after another tried to figure out what was going on. Then, finally, a diagnosis: that I had a rare arthritic condition, a brand of arthritis that would advance rapidly and, the experts said, kill me before I was 25 or 26. Though the diagnosis turned out, shortly thereafter, to be wrong, my world had been pulled out from under me.

The accurate diagnosis was far more mundane. I was simply wearing out my knees. Though I loved football, my legs were saying, even at my relatively young age, "Enough."

I resisted, and tried to take it easy, and somehow managed to play the rest of my junior and senior years, in a great deal of pain. I had some knee surgery — way more experimental in 1970 than it would be today, the first time it had been done at the University of Florida.

I actually had two good years, in terms of athletic performance and academics. I was recruited by the Dallas Cowboys and got accepted at Duke Law School. By the end of my senior year, though, there was no way I could think of playing pro football with my knees — at least not without a major rest in between.

The Cowboys and I came to an agreement that I'd do my first year at Duke Law School and then, the following year, if I could run the 40-yard dash at the same speed I could when they recruited me, I would join them.

Well, it never happened. I never did go back. I got so engrossed in academics that I decided to stay with law school. And to this day my knees aren't very good anyway. Would I like to have been a Dallas Cowboy? Of course. It would have been real nice to take it to that level. But sometimes that's just not the way life is.

Whatever happens though, and wherever you end up in life, you can't deny the role of mentors. One of the most important role models in my life was a coach I had in childhood, at the Northwest Boys' Club in Miami. It was a poor neighborhood, with lots of gritty kids, but the Boys' Club was a haven to us.

One of the coaches there, Rudy, was a single guy in his late 30s who had moved down to Miami from Rhode Island, and coaching kids was his life. He became a best friend to my dad, and became a part of our family — for our whole lives. He was even the best man at my wedding. He had his own home in Miami, but when he retired, he came to live with us. This was a guy who didn't have much in his life — he'd had a tough childhood, and no family of his own — but he was one of the richest men I've ever known.

Rudy loved sports, he loved kids and he loved fostering talent. There's no doubt about it, I simply would not have made All-American, or accomplished a lot of other things, without him in my life.

Contact Carlos Alvarez online at verizonreads.net/lifesplaybook.

SELF ESTEEM

"If you can wake up every day, look in the mirror and **like what you see, then you're halfway there** — and more likely than not, you're going to be successful."

JACK SIKMA

Self-Doubt

"I WRESTLE WITH IT EVERY DAY —
IS THIS WHAT I WAS MEANT
TO BE DOING? IS THIS
WHERE I BELONG?

IS THIS MY 'CALLING'?
IT CAN BE DEBILITATING.
BUT IT CAN ALSO
KEEP YOU HONEST."
MICHELLE JOHNSON

role model

"You don't have to know people personally for them to be role models. Some of my most important role models were historical or literary figures that I only read about — never actually met."
John Wilson

"The most important role models in people's lives, it seems, aren't superstars or household names. They're 'everyday' people who quietly set examples for you — coaches, teachers, parents. People about whom you say to yourself, perhaps not even consciously, 'I want to be like that.'"
Tim Foley

N U M B E R 1

Time out

A good role model doesn't have to be a media or sports superstar. He or she doesn't even have to be famous. Your role model can be someone in your family, school, workplace or community whom you respect and whose actions inspire you. The following questions may help you identify one or more real-life mentors in your world. You may want to write down your answers and put them away to review later.

1. Name someone you know who you respect and admire. Explain why.

2. Who in your life really motivates you to achieve? How do they do it?

3. Who do you wish you were more like? Who do you respect because of their relationships with others?

4. Name someone you know who has made sacrifices, either great or small, for a particular cause. What do you think motivates this person?

5. Name someone in your school, job, family or community about whom you can honestly say, "I'd like to be like him/her when I'm that age." Explain why.

6. If you're having difficulty naming someone in your life who truly motivates you to achieve, it's time to hit the books. A historical figure or even a fictional character can serve as a role model. Read some great works of fiction or biographies of distinguished individuals in history. Who inspires you? Explain why.

Visit Life's Playbook Online for more tips and resources: **verizonreads.net/lifesplaybook**

"Staying focused on what's important to me has allowed me to get to where I am."

STATS

- Political and social thought major, graduated from University of Virginia in 1981.
- Four-year starter and two-time Academic All-American for UVA women's basketball team.
- Received the Jettie Hill Award for the highest GPA among UVA women athletes.
- Graduated from UCLA Law School in 1985.
- Named Distinguished Alumna by the University of Virginia Women's Center in 1997.
- Currently president of the Women's National Basketball Association (WNBA).
- Named 1998 Female Sports Executive of the Year.

I think if there's one word that describes me best, it's probably "pioneer" — that's the aspect of myself that I'm most proud of.

I come out of what I've frequently called the Bronze Age — no, make that the Stone Age — of women's sports, a time when legislation for women's athletics was just taking effect, and when collegiate opportunities for women athletes were few and far between. And it wasn't even that long ago.

Though we've come a long way, and the existence and vitality of the Women's NBA today are amazing things, we've got a long way to go. I'm focused on the time when the WNBA will be the fifth major league — following men's basketball, baseball, football and hockey. I honestly think that could happen within the next decade.

Where I am now is a long way from my childhood of hanging a light bulb in the branches of a tree above my driveway in New Jersey, so I could shoot hoops at night, with gloves on my hands to keep them warm. I'd have to say that sports are probably in my genes.

Both my father and grandfather were high school athletic directors who encouraged my sports ambitions. But I always knew that sports success could never be at the expense of academics, and I took my college major in political and social thought — a combination of history, philosophy and political science — very seriously.

Graduating with the highest GPA among UVA women athletes was as important to me as what I achieved in basketball — and as for going to law school following a year of pro basketball in Europe, I always saw education as a key stepping-stone to a career in pro sports. Academics were always paramount to me.

Forging a career in pro sports wasn't easy. I still have the rejection letters I got from the NBA after applying for a job right out of law school. I had to work elsewhere, and still stay focused on where

Val Ackerman

I wanted to be, slowly working my way into the NBA as a staff attorney, then as special assistant to Commissioner David Stern. I have to say I never lost that focus.

I know that students today have it harder, in terms of staying focused, than my generation did. They have a lot more choices, good and bad, today, than we ever had — choices and distractions, everything from hanging out at the mall, to computers, to other entertainments — not to mention the pressures of sex, drugs and alcohol that my generation wasn't faced with in the same way.

I feel privileged to be right at the center of women's sports right now. It's a very exciting time — perhaps the most exciting time in our history. But it's staying focused on what's important to me that has allowed me to get to where I am — and that kind of focus can do the same for anyone.

Contact Val Ackerman online at verizonreads.net/lifesplaybook.

"You don't

aim

at the

bullseye.

You aim

at the

center

of the

bullseye!"

**Raymond
Berry**

TEAMWORK

"TO ME, A FAMILY IS JUST LIKE A TEAM — EVERYBODY'S GOT TO PLAY A PART, TO HOLD UP HIS OR HER END. SUCCESSFUL FAMILIES — AND TEAMS — ARE BUILT ON EACH MEMBER HELPING OUT THE OTHERS AS NEEDED." **Chad Hennings**

"Remember the little man sitting on the backboard."

STATS

- Graduated from University of Arizona in 1977.
- Played professional basketball for the New Jersey Nets, 1978-81.
- Earned MBA from Arizona and served on the faculty in 1986-87.
- Currently President and Owner of Robert A. Elliott, Inc., Accounting, Tax & Management Advisory Services, as well as a college and professional basketball analyst.

Twenty years ago, I had two major interests in my life: sports and accounting. And I'm very surprised that here I am today, with those two things still very much in my life — I'm a professional accountant, and I do sports broadcasting.

Accounting can be a very cold, impersonal thing — it's an isolating profession, just you and your computer sometimes. But for the "people" side of my personality, I've got sports. It's a great balance — and I always tell kids *that's* what they've got to find. But whatever you do, don't let parents, uncles, aunts, cousins tell you what to do. Honestly assess *yourself,* your interests, your abilities — and then "back into" a job or a profession that you'll honestly enjoy. That's the only way you'll thrive.

As independent as you have to be, though, it's funny the things that stay with you, things other people say that you remember your whole life.

Back in Ann Arbor, I had a junior high school coach named Mr. Anderson. He was an early mentor of mine, I guess you'd say, and has always been kind of proud of me because I was the first kid born and raised in Ann Arbor to play in the NBA. Anyway, I'll never forget how he taught me to make a lay-up shot.

Mr. Anderson used to say, "Just remember, there's a little man sitting on top of the backboard. If you throw the ball too high, or too hard, you're going to knock him off. But if you toss it up there just nice and soft, the little man will get it into the basket for you. Just let him help you."

Silly, I know, but it worked. And it still does — I use that same advice in coaching clinics today. To me, that's what learning is all about — seeing what people have to offer you, taking little bits of advice and information they provide, keeping it with you, then, if you're lucky, passing it on.

Contact Bob Elliott online at verizonreads.net/lifesplaybook.

"**Shoot** for the stars. You may not get the stars—but you may get the moon."

CARLTON YOUNG

STATS

- The first-ever woman Cadet Wing Commander and Rhodes Scholar at the U.S. Air Force Academy.

- Named AFA's Most Outstanding Scholar-Athlete and MVP in 1981. Earned the Military Performance Award in 1981.

- Earned a master's degree in political science and economics, Oxford University.

- Currently a U.S. Air Force Colonel and Deputy Group Commander at Altus Air Force Base, Okla.

- Speaks for many women's groups, including the Exchange Club, the Federal Women's Program and the USAFA Women in Leadership Symposium.

"I made a mistake during formation flying."

When I was growing up in Iowa, my parents had a little sandwich shop, with a parking lot out back where I used to shoot baskets. One day, as I was out there fooling around, a local coach saw me and stopped over. He asked if I could shoot left-handed. I said, "What?" He said, "You know, you *should* be able to shoot both left and right if you're serious about the game." He became a very supportive and knowledgeable mentor to me, and an example of what a good coach can be: a real motivator. I myself coached sixth-grade girls' basketball when I got older. Later, when I went back to the town after being away, very few girls were playing. They told me that it wasn't fun anymore. So many coaches forget that when they take the fun out of something, it's just not something people want to do.

But flying was *always* something that I loved to do, from the very first time. In training, though, I once made a mistake during formation flying, a fairly serious mistake. As a result, I had to have a formal academic review to see if I could continue to be allowed to fly. I passed the review without a problem and it showed me, as I've learned so many times in life, that it's in adversity that your true colors really shine through. I've always been someone who takes pleasure in being tested — and I mean that in every sense of the word — and in passing the test.

What would I have done differently in my life, if given the chance? I would have majored in physics in college, and maybe been a physicist. That's always fascinated me. I would also have pursued other, more "balancing" sports early on, sports that are more "life-long" than basketball: tennis, swimming, cross-country skiing, things I'm only now just getting into.

But you know what? Second-guessing your life and your decisions is good. All successful people I know have doubts and conflicts. Soul-searching is healthy. It keeps you honest with yourself.

Contact Michelle Johnson online at verizonreads.net/lifesplaybook.

Michelle Johnson

Knowing Who You Are and Why You're Here

"We need people in our lives who set standards and rules."

STATS

- Ranked second on Western Athletic Conference career-scoring list as an undergraduate at Brigham Young Univ.; won John Wooden Award as college basketball's Player of the Year in 1981.

- Made a last-second layup that upset Notre Dame in the third round of the 1981 NCAA tournament, which became one of the most famous shots in tournament history.

- Played pro baseball with the Toronto Blue Jays; drafted by the Boston Celtics in the second round of the 1982 draft. Played 14 years in the NBA — with Boston, Sacramento and Phoenix.

- Left to become head coach of Phoenix Suns, retired in 1999. Now working as analyst for Turner's NBA telecasts.

- Serves as a spokesman for the Children's Miracle Network; active with the Phoenix area Cystic Fibrosis Foundations and Stay-In-School Campaigns.

I admit it, I was lucky. I had a lot of support growing up. I had parents who taught me all about maintaining balance, and I grew up with the philosophy that to find fun and fulfillment in whatever your area of talent is — music or sports or chess — you have to have a sense of who you are, where you came from and why you're here.

When I think back, one of the things I'm most grateful for is that I had coaches who actually forced me to study. That may sound funny, but I use that word "forced" for a reason. Because that's what I needed. And it's what I think a lot of student-athletes need.

Athletics was something that always came naturally to me, but academics . . . well, I had to work hard at the academic side, both in high school and in college.

I had a high school basketball coach who was one of the sternest figures I've ever known. In fact, a lot of good players didn't even go out for basketball, for fear of having to play under this coach, his reputation was that intense.

What was most intimidating about him was that he had zero tolerance for slacking off academically. If you skipped one single class — you didn't get to play, and you didn't get to practice. Period. He had that kind of respect for academics, and was that unbending. Academic performance was mandatory, and there was no discussion.

Well, needless to say, I never missed a class. And it wasn't because I was such a dedicated student — I simply didn't want to jeopardize my basketball. I wanted to be able to play, and I didn't want that taken away.

My point is that we need people in our lives who don't necessarily crack a whip, but who set standards and rules that force us to discipline ourselves and perform up to a certain level. Let me assure you that those are some of the most important people in your life.

Contact Danny Ainge online at verizonreads.net/lifesplaybook.

STATS

- Graduated from Southern Methodist University with a degree in business administration, 1955.

- Drafted by the Baltimore Colts in 1955; helped the team to 3 NFL championships.

- Inducted into the Pro Football Hall of Fame in 1973.

- Coach of the New England Patriots from 1984-89; led Patriots to their first Super Bowl appearance, 1985.

- Currently serves on the Board of Directors of the Fellowship of Christian Athletes, the Alan Ameche Memorial Foundation, Tele-Missions International, Inc. and Bill Glass Ministries.

"Watch the ball into your hands."

Learning from your mistakes is a cliché, but in my life it's been a guiding principle. Let me give you an example — the biggest one I can think of.

My senior year in college — this was Southern Methodist University in the 1950s — we played a very critical game against the University of Texas. I personally fumbled the football twice in that one game — and we were in a good field position going into both of those plays.

Later on, we lost the Conference Championship and our Cotton Bowl berth by half a game. Even though responsibility for a loss is always shared, I felt totally responsible — even though, at the time, no one, including myself, realized how critical those two fumbles had been.

I never forgot that game. But from that point on, I had the memory of those fumbles branded on my brain so deep, I vowed it wouldn't happen again. And in the next 13 years I was charged with only one fumble — and the official blew the call on that one!

Did I learn from that mistake? You bet — not fumbling the ball practically became an obsession with me for the rest of my career.

I credit that game with teaching me the number-one fundamental a pass receiver must master. But I also remember learning one of the most important fundamentals in football from a piece of advice I "overheard."

When I was drafted by the Baltimore Colts in 1955, in a training camp locker room I heard someone talking about on old veteran receiver named Dan Edwards. These guys were saying that Edwards was someone who really understood football, and his philosophy for completing a pass was simply to "watch the ball into your hands."

That is a simple phrase, but very profound in a way — it's all about protecting the football, focusing on it, not breaking your

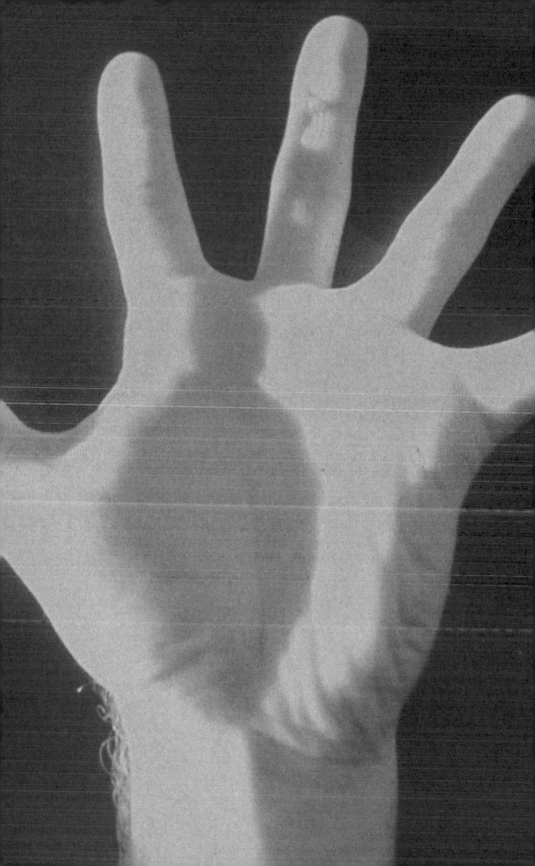

concentration even when the ball is nearly in your hands. To me that phrase crystallized everything you need to know about catching a football. And from that moment on, it became a part of my playing — and later, my coaching — philosophy.

Contact Raymond Berry online at verizonreads.net/lifesplaybook.

REACHING GOALS

"Never look down at your feet. **Always look ahead.** To be able to reach your goal, you have to be able to see it."

Tom McMillen

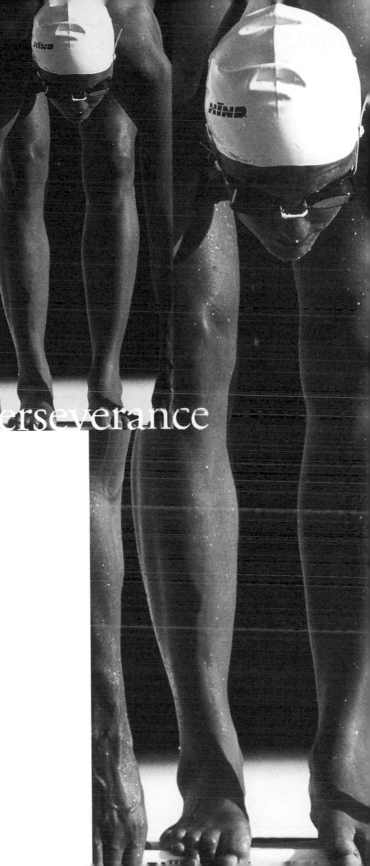

"Perseverance isn't just the willingness to work hard. It's that, plus the willingness to be stubborn about your own belief in yourself."

Merlin Olsen

Perseverance

WINNING

"ONE OF THE MOST IMPORTANT THINGS I'VE LEARNED FROM SPORTS IS THAT YOU JUST DON'T WIN EVERY GAME. AND YOU'RE NOT SUPPOSED TO. IT SOUNDS MUNDANE, BUT LIFE IS LIKE THAT. YOU'RE NOT SUPPOSED TO WIN EVERY GAME." LEE ROY SELMON

N U M B E R **2**

Everyone suffers disappointments and setbacks. But it's what you learn from the experience that counts. Being a perfectionist is commendable, but "perfect" people often have an unfortunate tendency to punish themselves when things go wrong. And things *will* go wrong.

Don't slam your fist into the wall the next time you're disappointed in your performance. Instead, take a deep breath, resolve to do better and sit down in a quiet place and write out some thoughtful answers to the following questions. Then file them away for future reference.

1. Was the failure caused by something I did — or was it completely out of my control?

2. Was I simply unprepared? Do I need to study or practice more?

3. Did I prepare too much? Was I too anxious to perform well?

4. Was I overconfident? Smug about my abilities?

5. How can I approach the same task next time and avoid making the same mistakes?

Visit Life's Playbook Online for more tips and resources: **verizonreads.net/lifesplaybook**

HALL OF FAME

Jolanda Jones

Telling the Truth

STATS

- Three-time NCAA heptathlon champion, two-time Academic All-American and a 1989 U.S. heptathlon champion.

- Won the high jump portion of the heptathlon event at the 1996 U.S. Olympic Team Trials, beating out even the legendary Jackie Joyner-Kersee.

- 1989 graduate of the University of Houston, magna cum laude and on the Dean's list with a degree in political science.

- Received a J.D. degree from the University of Houston Law School in 1995.

- In 2000, received the NAACP's Award for Legal Excellence for dedication to community service.

- Today, she is owner of the Jones Law Firm in Houston.

"The disadvantages and struggles associated with a childhood like mine don't have to

When I was working in corporate law a few years ago, representing wealthy individuals and corporations, I agonized over what I really wanted to do — to help people who, like me, had grown up poor.

After law school, I'd gotten caught up in the "get rich" mentality of many young lawyers and I was insecure about striking out on my own — with no guaranteed income or health benefits, and me a single mother with a young son to take care of.

After soul-searching for over a year, I went to my grandmother, whom everybody in my family knows as "Dear," and explained how terrified I was. Dear looked at me and said simply, "Sweetheart, you've always succeeded at whatever you set your mind to. There's no doubt

lead to welfare, prison or worse. You can learn positive things from adverse situations."

in my mind you'll succeed in your own law practice."

She didn't need to say anything else. As simply as that, the albatross was lifted. My confidence soared. Within a week, I resigned and began my happy, exciting, scary new life as my own boss. I've never looked back.

Confidence. That's what it takes sometimes to overcome seemingly insurmountable odds.

For me those odds included a father who committed suicide when I was a baby. An inner-city childhood of punishing poverty. Shared responsibility for taking care of four brothers and sisters, while my

Jolanda Jones
and grandmother "Dear"

mother worked long hours. And the loss of more than one member of my family to the violence of the streets.

But with a strong mother who taught me to stand up for what was right, and a grandmother who gave me a faith in myself and in God, I made it through.

No matter how hard I had to work, I wasn't going to let circumstances deny me things like straight A's in high school. Setting the Texas record as the only athlete, male or female, to win a state team championship as an individual. Qualifying for the final Olympic Trials as a teenager. Graduating from college magna cum laude with a Rhodes Scholarship nomination. And garnering an unprecedented three NCAA heptathlon titles in four years.

My mother once told me that although she couldn't afford to pay my way through college, my brain could, and she was right. Sure, there were some long, dark nights, I won't lie. Believe me when I tell you, anybody who strives to achieve anything meaningful in life eventually finds her or himself standing alone — sometimes grappling with feelings of self-doubt, sometimes wondering if it's all worth it.

I'm here to tell you it is.

I've built a career and a life on being involved, ambitious and committed — committed to others, and to myself. I'm building a business on helping those less fortunate, and, like my activist mother was in the 1960s, I'm a political person — as well as a brutally honest one. As the writer Grace Paley once said, "The most political thing you can do is to tell the truth."

Contact Jolanda Jones online at verizonreads.net/lifesplaybook.

LEARNING FROM SPORTS

"PLAYING AND COACHING SPORTS OVERSEAS HAS TAUGHT ME THAT SPORTS ARE A WONDERFUL BRIDGE BETWEEN AND AMONG PEOPLE. SPORTS ELIMINATE CULTURAL BARRIERS — YOU'RE EQUAL ON THE PLAYING FIELD." JOHN FOWLER

HALL oF FaMEr

Failure and "The Process"

STATS

- Graduated from Notre Dame in 1974 with a degree in economics.
- Had a 10-year NFL career, including 5 all-pro years and a Super Bowl championship with the Oakland Raiders.
- Serves on the Board of Directors of Minnesota Dollars for Scholars and works as a special agent for Northwestern Mutual Life.

"Failure is not an option."

To look at me when I was young, you'd have thought I was the least likely kid in the world to grow up and spend 10 years in the NFL.

I had several hernia operations before I was 10, so I couldn't really even get into sports before then. And on top of that, my dad wasn't particularly supportive of my going out for athletics.

I had a friend, though, who played Pee Wee Football. One day I was hanging out with him, watching practice, and later I came home and mentioned it to my mother. It was she who suggested I try out.

Anyway, the next day I stood around the practice field for what seemed like hours, until finally, someone asked me if I wanted to try out. I played in just blue jeans, shoulder pads and a helmet. On my first time out, I tackled one of the biggest guys. And although I really didn't enjoy all that hitting and crunching, I did what needed to be done.

It was Pee Wee Coach Robinson who got me to stick with it. He was the one who showed me that your job is to keep the coach quiet. If he's not screaming at you, you must be doing things right.

Coach Robinson taught me that success in sports, and in life, has to do with not accepting failure as an option. More important, he taught me that if you do fail, there's no sense blaming anyone but yourself. And that failing at something *once* isn't failure . . . it's just part of the process.

Contact Dave Casper online at verizonreads.net/lifesplaybook.

Making a Difference

"I wanted to spend my life doing something that

I had a privileged upbringing, no question about it. My dad had been an All-American at Cornell back in the 1930s. Back then, even though Ivy League football was on par with Ohio or Michigan, because of the color line in professional sports, Dad couldn't turn pro.

Rather than be bitter, he continued in education, got a master's from Cornell and his Ph.D. from University of Pennsylvania, and then went on to a distinguished career as a college president and, later, served as U.S. Ambassador to Sweden, appointed by President Nixon.

So you can imagine the raised eyebrows when I chose, after Harvard Law School, to turn my back on a corporate law career and

made a difference in the lives of others."

move to Harlem to start my own private practice and work on efforts to address the housing crisis in New York City.

The biggest lesson I've learned? You'd be surprised at the suspicions you arouse when you say no to options other people readily accept — indeed, aspire to. People couldn't understand why I, an upper-middle class African-American out of Harvard, would want to work with the homeless in Harlem. Some thought I was ridiculously overqualified. Some thought I had ulterior motives. Some thought I was a condescending "outsider." Some thought I was crazy, or that I just had it too easy.

That makes me laugh. People who think that All-Americans like me always had it easy should look at my college career!

First, against my parents' advice I went to the University of Michigan — I went there on a football scholarship my freshman year, with visions of a Big 10 career and playing in the Rose Bowl someday. I was miserable, and it didn't work out — I was the only

Joe Holland

player on the team from back East, and I was up against the whole midwestern alumni network. I felt like an outsider — and so I transferred to Cornell.

Then, when I got to Ithaca, I had to sit out a year because of the transfer rule. Later, unbelievably, when junior year kicked in and I could finally play, I got injured — a severe hamstring pull. The fact that I kept coming back too soon only aggravated it, and I spent my junior year in pain, mentally and physically. I *finally* got to play my senior year, but the twist was, I got played out of position — I was a tailback but I was the biggest back on the team, so the coach decided to play me at fullback. At that point, I felt like it was a miracle that I was playing at all!

But you know what? Perseverance is an important personality trait of mine, as I reflect on my life, whether it was football in college or the work I'm doing now. In both cases, deep down I knew I had the talent and the determination to make it work. And I knew it was what I wanted to do. And at the end of the day, that was really all that mattered.

As far as community service is concerned, I've always believed in the Biblical precept that to whom much is given, much is required. It's been a "given" to me that you share your wealth, your knowledge with those less fortunate. That's the basis of my work in Harlem today. Also, growing up in the 1960s, I was very much aware of racial and civil rights injustices, so it was natural that my community-service instincts would be channeled in that direction.

At one point, my parents lived in Yonkers, New York, and my sister lived on the Upper West Side of Manhattan. Driving down to visit my sister, I would go through Harlem, and that was my initial exposure to the area. Combined with a concentration in college on African-American History and my interest in "intellectual Harlem" — Marcus Garvey, Langston Hughes and the cultural heritage those figures represent — I made a connection to the place. So when it became clear that I wanted to spend my life doing something that made a difference in the lives of others, Harlem was it.

The rewards? They're incalculable. The greatest reward of my community service is seeing the changes in the lives that I've involved myself in. Watching individuals return to self-sufficiency and mental and physical health, after they've been living in the worst possible conditions — to see them going from sleeping on subways to being employed and spiritually "whole" — well, the satisfaction is beyond describing.

Contact Joe Holland online at verizonreads.net/lifesplaybook.

INSECURITY

"My theory is that most really successful people are fueled by an insecurity of some kind. I don't mean this in a negative way. Insecurity can be a great motivator."

Kermit Washington

"For me, reading was a refuge, and a ticket to where I wanted to go."

I'd have to say that, outside of my personal relationships, reading is probably the most important thing in my life.

As a shy, reserved kid who was overly conscious about his physical makeup — which I've written about in detail in years since — reading for me was an escape. It was a passage into a world where I could be comfortable, and flee my self-consciousness. And it was an entrée to a place where I could go to stimulate my mind, learn about new things, and satisfy my wanderlust and curiosity.

When I was a child, my family couldn't afford a TV. So our house was one of books and conversation. Because of my stuttering, I really only had two options — I could listen to others talk, or I could read! And since my mother was a librarian, she, of course, encouraged me to do the latter.

Even today, I try to read at least one book a week. My favorites are books on history, politics, travel and especially biography. For sports, I'm an inveterate reader of newspapers and magazines — I love the regular columnists and the theme pieces in the big national dailies. And I never miss an issue of the great sports magazines and journals.

Looking back on my career, though, I can remember knowing, and observing, athletes who simply hadn't been exposed to the rewards of reading.

So many aspiring athletes I knew made the mistake of thinking that they were going to get that big sports contract someday, and of assuming that their education didn't really matter.

You'd see them traveling to games, playing cards to kill time, when they could have been improving their minds. Even today, I'm shocked and saddened when I see high school, college and even pro athletes on buses and planes, traveling the circuit, playing video games or listening to their Walkmans, when instead they could enrich their lives, and train their minds, through reading. It's such a missed opportunity!

When I look back, my biggest regrets in life are missed opportunities. Also, it's ironic that athletes can be so interested in training their bodies, but often neglect training their minds. The best teachers I've

Bill Walton

ever had always taught me that the most important thing you could do in terms of training your mind was to "learn how to learn" — and you absolutely cannot do that without reading well.

The problem of low literacy is a major one, and it's a concern that spans the entire spectrum of our society. I have the same message for both young people and adults for whom reading is a challenge, and it's the same advice I have for anyone with a hurdle to surmount: you have to raise your fundamental skill level by working on your weaknesses. In our culture, not being able to read — and read well — is an enormous handicap. There's no getting around it.

The good news is that it's never too late to develop skills, in any field. There are certain skills you simply have to have, and if you've put off developing them, well, it's okay to let that go. But why not start now?

I've started learning all sorts of new things later on in life — gardening, music (the piano and drums) and computers to name a few. I'm not very good at any of them, but I never thought it was too late to learn a new skill. The same holds true for reading.

My life's experiences have taught me that reading puts you in control of your life, and brings enormous satisfaction. When I hear about a new book that piques my interest, there's nothing like the feeling of going online, ordering it and anticipating the pleasure it's going to offer in a free minute, evening or weekend.

I would encourage any student, of any age, to not just acknowledge the importance of literacy, but to get involved — whether it's through a volunteer organization, a local "literacy mentoring" effort, or another similar opportunity in your community.

Reading has shaped me more than anything else in my life — and has made me the person I am today. And anyone who has seen the volume and diversity of my home library knows that when I say that, I'm speaking from my heart.

Contact Bill Walton online at verizonreads.net/lifesplaybook.

LEARNING FROM SPORTS "I approach the O.R. to do an organ transplant

precisely the same way I used to step up to the blocks to run track: okay, I've got

to get from Point A to Point B — and I've got to do it right." CARLTON YOUNG

ACADEMICS

"I don't care how great you are in sports, if you're not cutting it as a student, you're not cutting it. I can't believe how many kids still believe you can make it on athletic ability alone." **Pat Richter**

"The major part of your life is going to happen after you're 25. Get your degree!" **Bernie Kosar**

N U M B E R **3**

Ask anyone — they'll tell you. It's easy to identify your dream, set your goal. But realizing it, reaching it step by step, day by day, is the hard part. How do you maintain your focus? The following questions may give you some food for thought on the road to reaching your dream.

1. Do you occasionally sit down and list the unpleasant tasks you've been putting off?

⭕ Yes ⭕ No

Suggestion: Make it a special point to tackle unpleasant jobs one by one. Check each off as you complete it. You'll be surprised at your feeling of accomplishment.

2. Do you do the things you like least "first thing"?

⭕ Yes ⭕ No

Suggestion: Procrastination causes stress and anxiety, and makes it harder to do the things you enjoy.

3. Do you remind yourself every day what your goals are?

⭕ Yes ⭕ No

Suggestion: This can be as simple as writing a few lines

in a notebook that you refer to as often as needed to keep yourself on track.

4. Do you ever visualize your success?

⭕ Yes ⭕ No

Suggestion: Take a few minutes each day and use your imagination. Picture yourself as confident, prepared. Put yourself on the mental starting line and imagine what it feels like to reach the finish.

5. Are you sure you're setting goals, not just "making wishes"?

⭕ Yes ⭕ No

Suggestion: A wish is a vague dream, while a goal is something we see in exact detail . . . along with a path on which to reach it.

6. Do you actively research ways to achieve your goals?

⭕ Yes ⭕ No

Suggestion: Make use of resources online or in your local library — check out biographies to learn how others have succeeded in achieving goals that are the same as or similar to your own.

Visit Life's Playbook Online for more tips and resources: **verizonreads.net/lifesplaybook**

"Frequently, the people most ready and willing to offer you advice are the ones least qualified to be giving it."
Michelle Johnson

"I'm not big on advice. Encouragement maybe, or understanding, sure. The ability to listen. But advice? Telling people what to do? It's a yawner."
Jack Mildren

"There are times when I've taken advice, certainly. But I'm more in favor of learning by watching others' successes and mistakes – and your own. Observing what works and what doesn't, and acting on it, is a lot more valuable than taking abstract advice."
Brock Strom

Hall of Fame

The Defining Moment

"My coach gave me the greatest gift anyone can give. He believed in me."

- Earned an electrical engineering degree from the University of Tulsa in 1968.

- Heisman Trophy runner-up who held 8 NCAA pass catching records.

- Played 11 years with the NFL's Miami Dolphins and was a member of 3 Super Bowl teams.

- While with the Dolphins, earned a master's degree in finance from University of Miami.

- Owned and managed 30 retail athletic footwear stores in Oklahoma, Arkansas and Texas for 15 years before selling his business in 1990.

- Financial consultant for Merrill Lynch.

Everyone experiences "defining moments" in their lives, an event or decision that has the power to completely change the course of your life by your response, either yes or no. Defining moments are often important and challenging opportunities that lay bare the pathway to success. And the decision to grasp your defining moment is almost always a struggle.

My first important defining moment occurred when I was 16 at Galena Park High School near Houston. I was a 141-pound second-team guard on the junior varsity. During a scrimmage against the varsity football team, one of the junior varsity's receivers was injured. The coaches asked for someone to volunteer. Terrified, I raised my hand — even though I had never once caught a pass in an organized football game. Well, I went on to catch six or seven passes in the remainder of the scrimmage. After the game, my coach, Jess Sadler, came up to me and said, "Howard, you sure can catch a football!" I didn't think much about it at the time, but my coach gave me the greatest gift anyone can give you. He believed in me.

I went on to a football scholarship at the University of Tulsa, where I was a consensus All-American and Heisman Trophy runner-up in 1965. I eventually ended up playing 11 seasons for the Miami Dolphins under perhaps the greatest coach in the history of the NFL, Don Shula — not to mention earning two Super Bowl rings.

When I was younger, I thought that the key to success was just hard work. But the real foundation is *faith*. Faith — the idea that "I can do it" — is the opposite of fear ("What if I fail?"). And faith creates motivation, which in turn leads to commitment, hard work, preparation . . . and eventually success.

But I always go back to that defining moment and how, if I hadn't raised my hand that hot August day in Houston as a kid, nothing might have come of me. To me, the most important thing in life is learning how to recognize a defining moment when it presents itself — and then knowing what to do with it.

Contact Howard Twilley online at verizonreads.net/lifesplaybook.

Ellen Mayer-Sabik

Athlete, Scholar, Doctor, Mom

STATS

- Phi Beta Kappa graduate of Cornell University, 1984.
- 1984 New York State champion gymnast in the vault and second in the balance beam.
- Attended Harvard Medical School; completed residency at Massachusetts General Hospital, where she was awarded a cardiac fellowship and became the attending physician at the emergency ward.
- Currently researching new advancements as a cardiologist at the Cleveland Clinic Foundation.

"Trying to excel in sports and academics simultaneously

I n college, I remember very clearly that I experienced academics as a respite, a relief from sports — and vice versa.

Pre-med and medical training are so tough, you have to put in so many hours, so intensely, that being in the gym for four hours straight working at gymnastics wasn't an obligation, it was a relief! Conversely, preparing for an academic exam required so much concentration that I literally couldn't think about gymnastics — I didn't have the time. So the two areas of my life definitely balanced each other. And frankly, they each took up so much time that I was forced to be incredibly efficient, just to do it all. I think that's probably what I learned most from trying to excel both in academics and athletics: the value of *efficiency*.

has always forced a balance in my life."

Of course, any working mother will tell you that, no matter how busy and full and demanding your life seemed in college, or graduate school, or in the early years of a career . . . once you have a child you really learn the meaning of not having enough time. I have two children now and sometimes, at the end of a long day, I have to laugh at how "busy" my life seemed before J.P. was born!

I had an incredible role model early on, though, in that sense — my mother is a cardiologist, and I was fortunate in growing up with a mom who successfully balanced being a doctor and a full-time mother, and who did it very well. Not many women of my generation had that kind of example set for them.

I'm also lucky in that I really love what I do. Today, as a cardiac

Ellen Mayer-Sabik and son J.P.

surgeon, working on echocardiograms and in a lot of other areas that require patient contact, I have the gift of being able to enjoy my patients. I spend a lot of time listening to them, explaining things, watching carefully how they react to good and not-so-good news. I really enjoy patient care — and I think that's what I like best about my job.

Contact Ellen Mayer-Sabik online at verizonreads.net/lifesplaybook.

ACCOMPLISHMENT

"Don't let what you cannot do **interfere** with **what you can do**."

JOHN WOODEN

"*Fear? You only fear what you can't control. My fears center on my kids. As they get older — they're all between 10 and 17 now — they're less in my control than they used to be. And what I fear is that I won't correctly teach them all the things they need to be happy in life. If I can do that, I feel I really will have accomplished something worthwhile.*"

Steve Taylor

"I love reading so much because it is an adventure.

Each time I pick up a book it takes me to places I've

never been before." *Joe Holland*

READING *reading*

"Reading challenges you to step outside your day-to-

day life and experience the lives of others — to know

the earth and its creatures, and then to wonder

about what's beyond." *Regina Cavanaugh Murphy*

Time management is nothing more than rating your obligations by their importance and allotting time accordingly. But what happens when everything in your life seems equally important? If your answer to any of the following questions is "Yes," there's room for time-management improvement in your schedule.

1. Are you involved in too many activities?

O Yes O No

Suggestion: If you're over-committed, think about cutting down. Do you really get satisfaction from each of these activities? If you're doing them from a sense of obligation, is that obligation really justified?

2. Is your social life suffering?

O Yes O No

Reminder: Being a worka-holic is no good. Time off from work, studying or prac-tice for rest and relaxation keeps you sane, and can help you perform better when you're "on."

3. Is your job affecting your school work?

O Yes O No

Suggestion: If you're a student and you have a part-time job, it's even more important to set and stick to a schedule for homework and studying every day. Alert your employer in advance if you think you'll need flexibility in your schedule.

4. Is your weekly calendar filled with non-academic activities?

O Yes O No

Reminder: Non-school and academic activities should have equal time. It's called balance.

5. Have you forgotten to make time for a non-academic, non-sports activity?

O Yes O No

Suggestion: Community volunteering? Peer counsel-ing? Family? Get "outside your box" — and make a contribution.

Visit Life's Playbook Online for more tips and resources: **verizonreads.net/lifesplaybook**

Success's *"Underlying Principles"*

STATS

- Two-time consensus football All-American at the University of Colorado.

- Nominated for the Heisman Trophy as a lineman.

- A 1963 graduate in physics; awarded a Rhodes Scholarship to Oxford where he received an M.S. in plasma physics. Went on to earn a Ph.D. in astro-geophysics from Colorado.

- Member of the Voyager Science Team; teaches astronomy part-time. Part-owner of Ponderosa Associates; consults on fires and explosions.

"I'm a scientist. I need to understand myself, others, the world, in that way."

You know, men often point to their fathers, or to a coach, as the primary inspiration in their lives. But I have to say that mine was my mother.

I came from an unconventional upbringing, back in Missouri. My parents were never married, and I was raised by a single mother long before it was common, or fashionable, to be one. My mom was an independent woman, a registered nurse, and she did the childrearing pretty much all by herself.

With the wisdom of the years — and I'm talking about looking back to the late 1940s and early 1950s — I can see now that my mom made an incredible difference in my life. Perhaps *the* difference. Not only did she believe in me, she made me believe in myself. She would give me books to read about historical figures like Alexander the Great, and tell me to imagine myself as one of them. Or she'd insist that I read books on astronomy, and then she'd ask me to teach *her* about the stars. She always encouraged a belief in my own competence and independence.

Mom had been raised on a farm, and so I spent a lot of time on my maternal grandparents' farm in Missouri; I guess you could say I had a kind of rock-solid midwestern upbringing in that sense.

I can even remember her putting me on a train, all by myself — I was probably going to see my grandparents — when I was only five years old. It seems inconceivable to me to do that today, and I remember her passing the conductor a $10 bill to look after me, but I felt ten feet tall.

I can't help but think she knew what she was doing in creating a very early independence in me — because Mom told me, one day when I was 10 or 11, that she was dying. She passed away when I was 15, and I know that the foundation she'd given me was what

made me tough, what got me through that early crisis and lots of others in my life.

Certainly, there have been other inspirational people in my life. My coach Tom Hancock at Lakewood High School was one. He had the incredible ability to bring out in me what I call a "will to power" with a single, motivating statement. I'll never forget when, giving our football team a pep talk, he looked at us and said, "There was a time when Lakewood went on the field and other teams feared them." That was all it took to gel us into action.

And there was my thesis advisor in college with his patience; and Roger Gallet, the co-inventor of the French atomic bomb, who made a big difference in my scientific career; and my wife, whom I credit, in the end, with much of the success I've had.

You know, even when I did my Ph.D. thesis on a really technical subject — a specific type of electromagnetic radiation generated by objects in the universe — I was determined to understand it from the perspective of basic physical laws. In other words, I'm always trying to get at, and understand, the underlying principles of things. Maybe because I'm a scientist, I need to understand myself, other people and the world in that same way.

Meanwhile, in my life, it's my mother whom I always look back on as the source of the underlying principles that make me tick!

Contact Joe Romig online at verizonreads.net/lifesplaybook.

NO EXCUSES

"AS A KID, I HAD THE GOOD LUCK OF HAVING A DAD WHO WAS A FORMER COACH — WITH A REAL 'COACH'S PERSONALITY.' THE EARLY REGIMENTATION I GOT FROM HIM HAS PROVEN TO BE A HUGE BONUS IN MY LIFE. ANY EXCUSE I HAD FOR NOT PERFORM-ING UP TO EXPECTATIONS . . . HE'D ALREADY HEARD IT!" JACK MILDREN

READING

"Literacy gives you confidence, rids you of self-doubt. Education has put me, a ghetto kid from a single-parent household, on a whole other level. There's no doubt in my mind that in our society, literacy is 'the great equalizer.'" **Jolanda Jones**

Is there such a thing as a "born leader"? Maybe, but more often leaders are singled out in a group because they help others work together more effectively. Take this quiz to see if you have what it takes to be a leader.

1. Do you regularly thank people who work with you on a project or assignment?

○ Yes ○ No

Suggestion: Sharing credit makes other people feel good *and* makes them more willing to help next time.

2. When trying to make a decision with a group, do you make time for everyone to share their opinion?

○ Yes ○ No

Suggestion: When people feel they have been part of a decision, they are more likely to work to support the decision or get the job done.

3. Are you open to criticism from others?

○ Yes ○ No

Suggestion: No one likes to hear criticism, but try to listen to what the other person has to say. Is there a message you can take away?

4. Do you inspire others with your own example?

○ Yes ○ No

Suggestion: Your own willingness to help on a project, even with some of the smaller or less fun tasks, will show that you care about getting the job done and inspire others to work harder too.

5. Do you like working with people who have backgrounds or styles that are different from yours?

○ Yes ○ No

Suggestion: Working with people from a broad range of backgrounds can increase creativity. Diversity in a group can open the door for ideas you may not have considered.

6. Do you volunteer to help others who could benefit from your experience?

○ Yes ○ No

Suggestion: Use some of your free time to help others. For example, if you're a proficient reader and enjoy teaching, become a literacy volunteer. You can find out more about literacy volunteer organizations through Verizon Literacy Network (verizonreads.net).

Visit Life's Playbook Online for more tips and resources: **verizonreads.net/lifesplaybook**

Jeannie Demers Henningsen

It's All About Support

"If I'm an example of anything, it's that ordinary people can —

- Played on the 1984 NCAA softball championship team. Selected as a GTE Academic All-America Team member four times as a two-sport athlete at Buena Vista University.

- Became the nation's all-time leading basketball scorer in the NCAA in all divisions by the end of her college career.

- Dean's list student for eight semesters and graduated in 1987 with a 4.0 GPA with a degree in elementary education.

- Currently an elementary school teacher in Iowa.

- Involved with her church and with Little League baseball and volleyball; coaches basketball and volleyball at elementary, high school and college levels.

You could say that mine was sort of a storybook, midwestern childhood, I suppose.

We lived on a farm in Iowa, where my mom still lives, and I teach elementary school in a town right next door. I've known my husband since we were in kindergarten together.

But despite how traditional and apple-pie it all sounds, right from the beginning I was used to not letting barriers stand in my way. And what was great was that my parents encouraged that.

For instance, there was no girls' Little League in Storm Lake, Iowa, when I was growing up. But my dad, who was a farmer, and

with lots of support from those around them — accomplish extraordinary things."

anything but an activist, had absolutely no problem taking me over and asking the boys' Little League coach if I could be on the team.

Despite what you hear about people being closed-minded sometimes, the coach — wisely — said yes. It didn't hurt that I was better than most of the boys.

Well, that was the beginning of a long career of achieving things in sports — and in the classroom — not only because I believed in myself, but because other people believed in me too.

I've always been lucky to have that kind of support — whether it was from my siblings, with whom I grew up playing softball and basketball, or great coaches in high school and college, who not only

encouraged and lit a fire under me, but helped me prioritize and balance school and athletics. I also had the love and encouragement you get when you grow up in a small town where everyone knows you, and cares about you your whole life.

Sometimes I look back at college, where I somehow maintained a 4.0 grade-point average while playing basketball, and I wonder how the heck I did it.

Then I remember all the countless games and practices my mom and dad drove me to, never complaining. I remember coaches like John Naughton and Marge Willadsen at Buena Vista University — folks who you could not only turn to anytime you needed something, but who were as excited as you were when you won a game or broke a record.

One of the great things about setting records and being recognized for it, like I have been, is that you get to experience the love and support you receive from people when, as an ordinary person, you accomplish something extraordinary. The pleasure that other people take in sharing your achievement never ceases to amaze me.

As a teacher, I try to instill feelings of possibility and potential for greatness in my students, young as they are. But as the product of a small town, I know that lots of support is what really makes greatness possible.

Contact Jeannie Demers Henningsen online at verizonreads.net/lifesplaybook.

STANDING OUT

"I OFTEN SEE SCHOLARS, ATHLETES, ARTISTS, MUSICIANS, STUDENTS WHO ARE GIFTED BUT WHO ARE AFRAID TO STAND OUT ... WHO DON'T WANT TO TRY TOO HARD, SHINE TOO BRIGHTLY, BECAUSE THEY'RE AFRAID OF NOT BEING COOL. THEY 'LAY BACK IN THE WEEDS' BECAUSE THEY'RE SELF-CONSCIOUS, OR AFRAID OF NOT BLENDING IN. FEAR AND SELF-CONSCIOUSNESS PARALYZE YOU ... AND CAUSE YOU TO FADE INTO THE BACKGROUND. AND THAT'S NO WAY TO EXCEL."
RON PERRY

"Reading is what

to achieve. Peopl

are confident in

simply because r

everywhere. Don

if you don't read

would like to. I'r

now than I was

practiced, and I

I didn't understa

as allowed me

who read well

aspects of life,

ding is necessary

be ashamed

well as you

a better person

en I started out.

sked questions if

l."

Jolanda Jones

"Reputation is what you're perceived to be. Character is what you really are."

STATS

- A standout basketball player for Purdue from 1930-32, he was the national player of the year in 1932, a 3-time All-American and captain of the 1932 Big 10 and National Championship team.

- Coached UCLA to 10 NCAA basketball championships, including a record 7 in a row (1967-73).

- Was named college Coach of the Year 6 times during his 27 years at UCLA. Coaching record was an astounding 885-203, a .813 winning percentage.

- Retired, lives in Encino, Calif.; active in church work and speaking engagements through John Wooden Enterprises. Donates most of his honoraria to charities and churches.

- Author of several widely distributed books dedicated to educational and motivational messages, based on his "Pyramid of Success."

Success and achievement in life have so much to do with *character* — and yet character is so hard to define. In my mind, it's simply having an innate sense of the right thing. The right thing to do, the right thing to say, the wise decision to make.

To me, someone with character is someone who can be trusted with anything. Who can be relied upon to know the proper thing to do in any situation. And character, to my mind, is something that's formed early. In youth. Maybe even in preschool days.

What I've always tried to get across, both to my own kids and to anyone I've ever coached, is the difference between character and reputation. Reputation is what the world sees in you — the way outsiders perceive you to be. Character, on the other hand, is what you know *yourself* to be. And often, the two can be very, very different. Contradictory, even. It's character, of course, that's far more important — although we seem to worry more about what others think of us than what we think of ourselves.

As I look back on my coaching career, two observations come to mind.

The first is that I'm more and more convinced that really good coaching is based purely in leadership and a positive example — not fear and intimidation. So many coaches, even big-name coaches, use fear-based tactics to ride herd on their team. And they're successful, frequently — they have great results. But I'm convinced that they would have had the same results, maybe even better ones, by using a more positive approach. Good coaching is about leadership and instilling respect in your players. Dictators lead through fear — good coaches do not.

The second observation is the irony that, while individual athletes, both college and professional, have gotten better over the

John Wooden

years — athletes are better, bigger, stronger, more skilled now than they were 30 or 40 years ago, without doubt — team play has, in fact, *declined*.

To me, this is a direct result of the "star" or "celebrity" mentality in sports — the worship of the individual over the team. Perhaps it's a function of media coverage, or advertising and promotion, or the general cult of celebrity in our culture, but we've sacrificed a lot in losing our sense of team.

As individual athletes achieve more and more, become better and better known, make more and more money, the awareness of the importance of team-work and unity is evaporating, and I think it's a bad thing. We've got to get refocused on the value of the team.

Contact John Wooden online at verizonreads.net/lifesplaybook.

"THERE ARE THINGS IN YOUR LIFE YOU CAN CONTROL — AND THERE ARE VARIABLES YOU CAN'T. THE MORE DILIGENT YOU ARE AT CONTROLLING WHAT YOU CAN, THE MORE INFLUENCE YOU'LL HAVE OVER YOUR DESTINY. YOU JUST HAVE TO FIGURE OUT WHICH ARE WHICH." *CARLTON YOUNG*

Control

"MY WHOLE LIFE, MY DREAM WAS TO BE PART OF SOMETHING SPECIAL. I NEVER REALLY HAD ANY INTEREST IN BEING A STAR — I JUST WANTED TO PLAY ON A GREAT TEAM." BILL WALTON

TEAM
WⓄRK

HALL oF FAME

Track Stars and Transplants

STATS

- Graduated from Villanova University in 1983 with a B.S. in biology.

- Three-time All-American in track at Villanova.

- The second-fastest 400-meter runner in school history with a career-best time of 45.32 seconds.

- Graduated from Johns Hopkins Medical School in 1987, and earned a transplant surgery fellowship to the University of Wisconsin.

- Currently assistant surgeon of transplantation at Birmingham (Alabama) Hospital and one of the nation's leading authorities on transplant surgery.

"Transplant surgery is a funny business."

In 1995, after finishing my transplant surgery fellowship, rather than join an established transplant surgery program at one of our nation's major medical centers, I decided to go to the University of Arizona, where I had an offer to establish my own pancreas transplant program. It turned out to be the most challenging experience of my life — and I attribute my ability to endure it to what I learned in sports.

Transplants are a funny business — they're based very much on supply-side economics. There are a limited number of organ donors and many more patients waiting for those organs. This makes establishing a successful program difficult. The pressure, financial and otherwise, was enormous.

In addition to teaching me a lot about my own cognitive and surgical abilities, the experience of struggling to launch that program taught me a lot about diligence, enduring difficult times, and what you can accomplish with determination. In my darkest moments, I would think about one of my many role models, Coach Jumbo Elliott at Villanova.

I'm not exaggerating when I say that in college, every time we stepped on the track, we ran not only for Villanova, but for Jumbo Elliott. He was tough, tough as nails. But in track everybody was gunning for Villanova back then, and we didn't want to let Coach Elliott down. Every member of the team felt that way. And we knew that by performing well individually, we would perform well collectively. In many respects, this is true for a medical team as much as it is for a track team.

Nevertheless, despite high hopes, everyone has his or her setbacks. Coming out of high school, I ran against Carl Lewis — and won. But then genetics kicked in, and Carl improved in college and evolved into the greatest sprinter in history.

As for me, I suffered a serious hamstring injury that destroyed my hopes of becoming a world-class sprinter. I then moved to the

Carlton Young

400 meters, which meant learning a new event. Though it wasn't my favorite, I persevered. Even though I was unsure if I could be as successful in the 400 meters as I was in the 100 meters, I did my best to achieve. I won the NCAA indoor title in 1983, but the 1984 Olympics were not to be mine. Was I disappointed? Sure. But facing a new challenge and succeeding is what life is about.

Contact Carlton Young online at verizonreads.net/lifesplaybook.

Did you ever hear of the Six W's?

"PERSISTENCE

'WORK
WILL
WIN
WHEN
WISHING
WON'T.'

Todd Blackledge

If it's not fun, do you really want to do it? Lighten up! There's nothing noble about being a martyr to the cause of a winning season or perfect grades or an insane work schedule. Try the following to help you relax.

1. Keep a stress diary.

Maintain a written record of stressful situations: what caused them, how you reacted, what physical symptoms you noticed. On a periodic basis, review your diary. See if you can discover patterns and figure out ways you can avoid stress "triggers." It's also a great way to review how you resolved stressful situations in the past and to realize that you can overcome challenges you face.

2. Learn to breathe.

Five minutes of quiet meditation each day, during which you concentrate on breathing slowly, rhythmically, deeply and from the diaphragm, will help you relax significantly.

3. Practice "body scanning."

Lie flat. For ten minutes, mentally "scan" your body, starting from the toes and moving up. Identify areas where you feel anxiety has tightened your muscles and, while deep-breathing, concentrate on letting go of the tension. Try to visualize the tension leaving your body.

4. Establish "relaxation triggers."

Choose a personal visual or behavioral trigger that, whenever you experience it, "cues" you to relax. It could be "Every time I see a stoplight," or "Every time I hang up a phone."

5. Don't hold on to anger or resentment.

They build up. If you have a conflict or disagreement with a friend, teammate, teacher or colleague . . . deal with it. Don't be combative, but assertive and reasonable. Ideally, it'll end in compromise. But don't wait.

6. Attack the source of your stress.

Sometimes, stress in our lives is caused by things that, with some effort, we can control – a substance abuse problem, an eating disorder, low literacy. If this is the case, take charge! Don't let a solvable problem cause undue anxiety. It might be an uphill battle at first, but in the long run, you'll save a lot of grief.

Visit Life's Playbook Online for more tips and resources: **verizonreads.net/lifesplaybook**

"In the public eye, you live your life with the knowledge that people are watching you. I try to balance marriage, children and job responsibilities as best I can — always trying to be sensitive to the impressions I make." **Val Ackerman**

"*I feel like I'm proof that ordinary people can grow up to do extraordinary things. If the kids I teach every day can absorb that piece of information, and use me as an example and maybe even an inspiration, then it's all worth it.*"

Jeannie Demers Henningsen

N U M B E R **7**

Time out

Being focused is great. Being passionate about something can be even better. But if you're so intense that you're stressed out and pre-occupied with one aspect of life to the exclusion of everything else, you're missing out.

Take a look at the list below. How many items can you check off?

Sometime within the last month, I . . .

___ Took a walk with no particular destination in mind.

___ Sat around with friends and talked about a current book, movie or music video.

___ Went to a sports event or some kind of performance as a spectator, not a participant.

___ Ate a leisurely dinner and stayed at the table afterward to talk with my family.

___ Read a magazine cover to cover, just for fun.

___ Spent a weekend without watching a single televised sports event or sitcom.

___ Looked up some information I was curious about, but didn't need for an assignment.

___ Got involved in a food drive or other charitable community effort.

___ Wrote a letter or made a phone call to an old friend.

___ Took time out to write a note or say thank you to someone who didn't expect it, but deserved it.

___ Listened — really listened — to a friend or family member tell me about their day.

___ Hung out with people who aren't involved in any way in the same work, school or activities as I am.

If you marked fewer than four items . . . you may want to think about "taking a break" and branching out!

Visit Life's Playbook Online for more tips and resources: **verizonreads.net/lifesplaybook**

Mistakes

"Our mistakes don't make or break us — if we're lucky they simply reveal who we really are, what we're really made of. I think that this is true whether it's a ball game and you're six points behind and it's 30 seconds to go, or something a lot more personal and serious. The bad times and the challenges will come. But if you treat them simply as tests of who you really are, you'll come out of them not bitter and victimized — but smarter and stronger."

Donn Moomaw

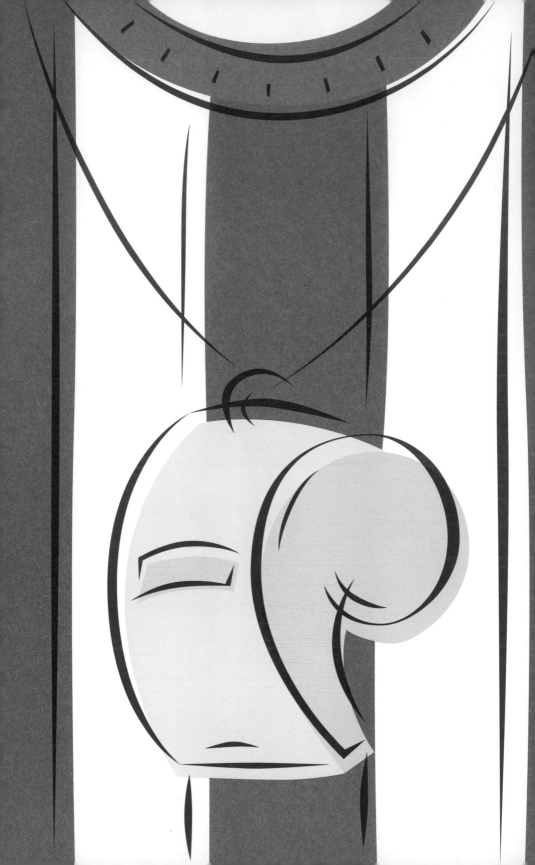

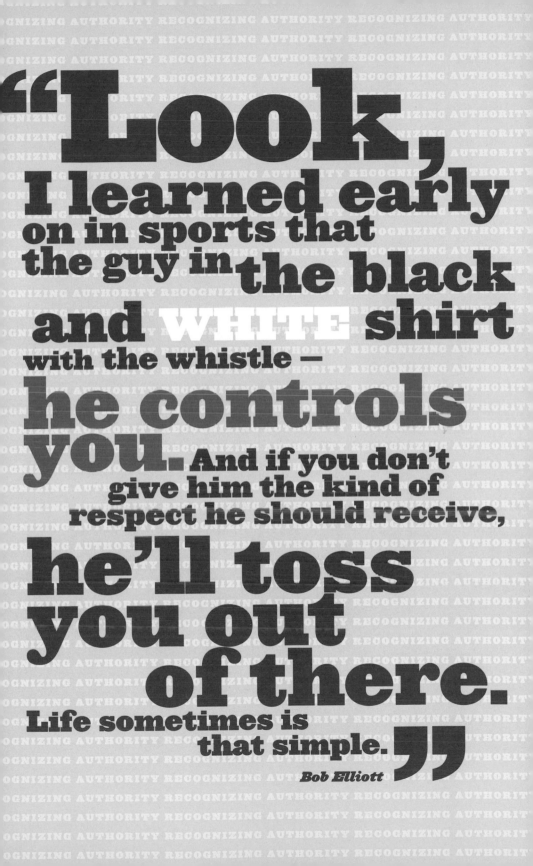

"**Look,** I learned early on in sports that the guy in the black and **WHITE** shirt with the whistle – he controls you. And if you don't give him the kind of respect he should receive, he'll toss you out of there. Life sometimes is that simple."

Bob Elliott

role

"You've got to be careful whom you pattern yourself after because you're likely to become just like them." *Rick Mayo*

"Somewhere along the line you have to trust someone. You've just got to be clever enough to pick someone who's smart and wholesome and worthy — and then just listen to what they say." *Dave Joyner*

"My dad passed away when I was five, and my mom was left with eight kids, of which I was the youngest. My mother's strength and determination have been an inspiration to me. You talk about a role model."
Anne Donovan

Confidence and Cold Sweats

- Consensus All-America tackle at Penn State, 1972. A pre-med major, he earned 3 varsity letters each in football and wrestling.

- Medical degree: Hershey Medical Center, Penn State, 1976.

- Currently serves as an orthopedic surgeon at 3 Pennsylvania hospitals.

- Served as Head Physician for the U.S. Olympic Team at the 1992 Olympic Winter Games in Albertville, France; chairman of the U.S. Olympic Committee's Sports Medicine Committee and vice chairman of the U.S. Olympic Committee's Anti-Doping Committee.

"I used to sit bolt upright at night with anxiety."

Everybody always says, "You can't be successful without making mistakes." "You learn from your errors." "Failure is how you make progress to the next level."

That's all well and good — until you start a business. As an orthopedic surgeon who's worked at three Pennsylvania hospitals and also served as head physician for the U.S. Winter Olympic Team (1992, Albertville), I launched a for-profit rehabilitation clinic several years ago. Overnight, I turned from a doctor to a doctor/businessman. And when the realities of revenues, expenses, profits and losses would run through my mind at the end of a long day, I'd wake up at night in a cold sweat, thinking, "My God, what have I done?"

In the morning, though, I'd remember what legendary coach Joe Paterno at Penn State always used to say to us: "Follow your instincts. Don't give up. Trust your gut. Be persistent." Eventually, the cold sweats got less frequent, and things were fine.

My point is that role models, and the advice they proffer, stay with you. Especially coaches — particularly the ones who see something in you that you don't even see in yourself.

When I was in my junior year in high school, I'd never played football or any sport, and I tried my hand at varsity wrestling. The wrestling coach, a great guy and former Penn State champion wrestler named Homer Bahr, called me over, looked me in the eye and said, "Son, if you stay after practice every day, work hard and stick with it, you will be a state wrestling champ someday." He didn't even know me.

I didn't believe him, of course, but because he believed in me, I started doing it. He nearly killed me with training and hard work, but, because of his confidence in me, I stayed with it. Not long after, I wrestled in a scrimmage meet against the state discus champion.

Dave Joyner

He pinned me in about 13 seconds. It was humiliating. But still, I stayed with it. In February, three months later, I wrestled the same guy for the district championship . . . and won.

You know, if you read a biography of Abraham Lincoln — or many great figures in history — one of the most startling observations is the number of things they *failed* at before achieving success. The ability to outwork the other guy, and sheer persistence, will usually lead to success — but frequently only after many failures. You can't forget about that, and you can't be discouraged by it.

Another thing I try to remember is that success is a way to measure yourself against yourself — not against other people. You tell me who's more successful — a carpenter who earns $20,000 a year making wonderful, satisfying pieces of furniture, out of love and craftsmanship . . . or the CEO of a billion-dollar company whose life is in a shambles, who drinks too much and who has trouble sleeping at night because of the pressure?

Contact Dave Joyner online at verizonreads.net/lifesplaybook.

READING

"'Reading' is much more than opening a book or a newspaper. It is drinking from the common cup of knowledge and experience accumulated over the centuries by our ancestors."
OLIVER LUCK

"YOU'VE GOT TO KEEP THE UPS AND DOWNS IN YOUR LIFE IN PERSPECTIVE. LOOKING BACK, IN THE BEST YEAR OF MY LIFE, MOST OF MY TIME WAS SPENT STRUGGLING TO GET THINGS DONE — THINGS WEREN'T ALL THAT GREAT, THEY ONLY ARE IN RETROSPECT. AND IN THE WORST YEARS OF MY LIFE ... WELL, LOOKING BACK THINGS WEREN'T ALL THAT BAD."

DAVE CASPER

THE ROLE OF SPORTS

"THE BIGGEST LIFE LESSON TO BE LEARNED FROM SPORTS: YOU'RE GOING TO HIT HURDLES, YOU'RE GOING TO LOSE, YOU'RE GOING TO FAIL SOMETIMES. THEN WHAT? IT'S WHAT YOU DO WITH THAT FAILURE — WHAT YOU LEARN FROM IT, WHAT YOU CREATE OUT OF IT — THAT MATTERS." BOB THOMAS

When we perform well at something, it's sometimes hard to describe how we do it. "It just happens naturally," we might say. But in reality, we're processing information all the time. In this exercise, use "sensory recall" to uncover clues from your past performance that you can use again in the future.

1. Go to a quiet place. (With practice, you'll be able to do this exercise anywhere.)

2. Remember a specific time and event when you performed really well at something — maybe you hit a great shot in tennis, participated in an interesting group discussion or did well on an assignment or test. Review the event in your mind as if you're watching a movie of it.

3. Try to remember the exact sensations you experienced — what you heard, saw and felt at that moment. Focus specifically on these "internal" reactions and try to block out other people and distractions that might have been present.

4. Run the "movie" back through your mind several times. Try changing some of the sensory details to test your memory. For example, vary the sounds from loud to soft, the images from color to black-and-white, your feelings from relaxed to tense, slow to fast.

5. Decide what you consider to be the important details of the experience — images, colors, sounds and feelings that you felt most strongly.

6. Repeat steps 1 to 5, but this time focus on something you did that was not successful. Relive the experience in the same way, and compare the images, sounds and feelings that come to mind to the clues you identified from the successful experience. How are they similar or different?

7. Record your conclusions about both your successes and disappointments in a journal for future reference. Reread what you wrote frequently to build your confidence in your hidden strengths and to help keep track of those areas you may need to work on.

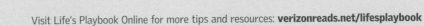

Visit Life's Playbook Online for more tips and resources: **verizonreads.net/lifesplaybook**

Trust Your Instincts—And Your Mentors

"The best mentors are the people in your life who push you just a little bit

The word "tomboy" is something you don't hear very much these days — it's a bit politically incorrect, I guess. But that's definitely what I was. And you know, it wasn't all that accepted for a girl to be as athletically inclined as I was as a kid. But I was lucky enough to have parents who encouraged me to pursue my athletic interests. My folks never dissuaded me from my interest in sports — which was kind of unusual.

I can't help comparing it to today, where things have really changed, and girls' athletics have become a totally accepted part of society. I marvel at how young women of all ages nowadays have access to a range of intramural sports — basketball teams, softball

outside your "comfort zone.'"

teams, soccer, even ice hockey! Things have evolved dramatically, and I think it's great.

When I was in high school, my dream was to go to a Division I school and play basketball. A lot of people — friends in high school — told me to forget it. But my instincts told me I could do it, and that I *could* balance academics with serious athletic ambitions. So I went to Connecticut against a lot of people's advice, and it turned out to be the best thing I could have done. It taught me a lot about just following your instincts — knowing what's right for you.

Similarly, going into medicine was an example of following my gut. I just pursued what my interests were — the biological sciences, particularly microbiology. I wasn't an active pre-med, just a dedicated science major — a typical athlete with interests in physiology, physical therapy, health sciences, injuries and illnesses. When I decided at the last minute to apply to medical school, I limited

myself to local schools in my area, and schools I was familiar with — Pittsburgh, Penn State, University of Connecticut.

I have to credit Dr. Theodore Taigen, in whose lab I did my honors thesis, with pushing me. He said, "Why not Harvard? Why not Johns Hopkins?" The embarrassing thing is, when he said that, I have to admit I didn't even know where Johns Hopkins was! I'd never heard of it — total ignorance! Dr. Taigen even said he'd pay for the application.

Well, just to make him happy, I applied. I was so close to the deadline that the only photo I had of myself, which was required with the application, was a shot of me standing in front of a waterfall at Disney World in a UConn t-shirt. Well, I got in. And today, I'm practicing surgery — and pioneering an area for women in medicine that I love.

The best news is that I've stayed in close contact with Dr. Taigen. Still a biology professor at Connecticut, he's very involved in the honors scholar program and a wonderful person in my life. He always pushed me outside my comfort zone all through college, and was the one person in my life who kept telling me I could "do it." That I *could* handle the University Scholar program. That I *could* complete my research. That I *could* make it to Hopkins.

And he was always right.

Contact Leigh Curl online at verizonreads.net/lifesplaybook.

N U M B E R 9

No one understands the importance of reading in enriching your perspective, and your life, like the members of the Verizon Academic All-America Hall of Fame. So what are they reading? And what do they recommend *you* read? Check it out!

John Fowler: *20,000 Leagues Under the Sea, From the Earth to the Moon,* and *Around the World in 80 Days,* all by Jules Verne

Jeannie Demers Henningsen: *To Kill a Mockingbird,* by Harper Lee

Bill Walton: *Undaunted Courage,* by Stephen Ambrose • *The Children,* by David Halberstam • *The Origin,* by Irving Stone • *The Bonfire of the Vanities,* by Tom Wolfe • *Two Tears Before the Mast,* by William H. Dana • *Go Up for Glory,* by Bill Russell • *The Fatal Shore,* by Robert Hughes

Jolanda Jones: *For Colored Girls Who Have Considered Suicide — When the Rainbow Is Enuf,* by Ntozake Shange • *Slaves in the Family,* by Edward Ball • *Brothers and Sisters,* by Bebe Moore Campbell

Pat Haden: *No Such Thing as a Bad Day,* by Hamilton Jordan • *The Tipping Point: How Little Things Can Make a Difference,* by Malcolm Gladwell • *The Greatest Generation,* by Tom Brokaw • *The Big Sleep,* by Raymond Chandler • *All I Really Need to Know I Learned in Kindergarten,* by Robert Fulghum • *The Russia House,* by John LeCarré

Oliver Luck: *The Forty Days of Musa Dagh,* by Franz Werfel • *Ghosts of Cape Sabine,* by Leonard F. Guttridge • *How the Irish Saved Civilization,* by Thomas Cahill • *The Diary of Adrian Mole,* by Sue Townsend • *Notes From a Small Island* and *A Walk in the Woods,* by Bill Bryson

Anne Donovan: *Wish You Well,* by David Baldacci • *Piercing the Darkness* and *The Prophet,* by Frank Peretti

Carlos Alvarez: *Gandhi: A Life,* by Yogesh Chadha • *Episodes of the Cuban Revolutionary War, 1956-58,* by Ernesto Che Guevara

Visit Life's Playbook Online for more of the Hall of Famers' recommendations:
verizonreads.net/lifesplaybook

NUMBER **10**

Substances that stimulate — or relax — are sometimes tempting to high-performing, highly pressured scholars and athletes. But think about the following. . . .

- **FACT.** We don't necessarily do better work on coffee. Caffeine increases speed, but not mental power or acuity. It can also cause jitters, elevate your blood pressure and increase lactic acid levels.

- **FACT.** Caffeine cannot sober up a drunk person — it has no counter-effect whatsoever on alcohol.

- **FACT.** Livelier behavior from drinking alcohol is due to the "stupefication" of the higher brain functions that normally control social behavior and inhibitions. As more alcohol is consumed, the other, more basic functions of the brain are increasingly affected — in turn causing lack of physical, verbal and mental coordination.

- **FACT.** One serving of alcohol can have more than 150 calories — it is a frequent cause of obesity in people who otherwise don't overeat.

- **FACT.** Alcohol causes fluid loss and robs the body of its ability to stay cool.

- **FACT.** Nicotine is an alkaloid, a naturally occurring compound. A dose of 60 mg — half of what is found in a normal cigar, and the amount in two to three cigarettes — is sufficient to kill a person in minutes. The fact that people survive smoking at all has to do with the body's ability to metabolize and break down nicotine and eliminate it, especially when the nicotine is ingested over a long period of time.

- **FACT.** Carbon monoxide and hydrogen cyanide, both breakdown products found in tobacco smoke, bind to hemoglobin irreversibly. The affected red blood cells can no longer carry oxygen. And lack of oxygen can permanently kill brain cells.

Visit Life's Playbook Online for more tips and resources: **verizonreads.net/lifesplaybook**

"IT TAKES A LOT MORE THAN A GAME TO SHAPE SOMEONE'S CHARACTER —
BUT A GAME PROVIDES AN ENVIRONMENT IN WHICH THE GOOD
QUALITIES IN A PERSON'S CHARACTER CAN RESPOND." *MARV LEVY*

CHARACTER

Ch

"A baseball coach once told me that success in life boils down to four simple rules: 'Be on time, wear your uniform, don't throw rocks, and stand up in the outfield."

Bob Elliot,

- Graduated from Utah State in 1962, the school's top male business student and the 1961 Outland Trophy winner as the nation's top collegiate interior lineman.

- Selected for the Pro Football Hall of Fame in 1982, as well as for the college Football Team of the Century and the NFL's 75th Anniversary Team.

- Has been a television analyst for both NBC and CBS; spokesman for FTD since 1983.

- Noted network television actor who devotes time to many charities. Host of the Children's Miracle Network since 1983. Member of the board of the Southern California Multiple Sclerosis Society; named National Winner of the 1981 Outstanding MS Volunteer Award. Works with Child Help, for battered and abused children in Southern California.

"Athletics came hard to me. In high school, my coach advised me to play on

When I was a kid, the sad fact was that I simply didn't have the coordination or basic skills that most "natural athletes" have, and whenever I tried out for a team, I was inevitably one of the first players rejected.

But it was when I went out for the basketball team in the ninth grade — not football, but basketball — back in Logan, Utah, and I almost got myself killed that the coach, genuinely puzzled, asked me flat out: "Why are you *doing* this to yourself?" The only answer I could give him was that perseverance was part of my personality.

"We're in the process of developing athletes for the high school," I remember the coach saying, "and you're not going to be one of

my musical talent and join the band."

them." I think he was honestly concerned about my getting hurt.

I didn't give up. Finally, when I was a sophomore, I made the football team. It wasn't luck, or skill, particularly — but sheer perseverance. And it wasn't just the willingness to work, it was a stubbornness I had, a trait that I can only conclude is innate. It's a characteristic that I'd say has served me well.

Does perseverance always pay off? Of course not. There are a dozen things I could point to in my life, not just failures but mistakes, blown opportunities, wrong turns, where I just wanted to put my head down and cry.

One of the things in my life that I will always have painful recollections of is the fact that my teams never did well in the NFL play-

offs. We had so many near-misses — in fact, I played on teams that ended the season one game short of the Super Bowl on three different occasions — which has got to be some sort of a record. Could I have done things differently? Maybe. Was it partly just a roll of the dice? Probably. But you can't look at those things as the end of the world.

One of the big myths of sports — and this is the way a lot of athletes live their lives, unfortunately — is, "Gee, if I can just win the championship . . . be the most valuable player . . . walk off with the gold medal . . . my life will somehow be different, and everything will begin again."

The reality is, it won't. Would my life be dramatically different today if I'd won a Super Bowl ring? Probably not. You've got to keep things in perspective — and that's what keeps you *balanced*. That's the real magic word.

Contact Merlin Olsen online at verizonreads.net/lifesplaybook.

"Our society is so **caught up in winning**, we forget that most of the **great men and women in history have, at one time or another, failed at something**. Often repeatedly, and discouragingly. But each failure is nothing more than a brick in the wall that forms the foundation of our success. We can't forget that."
Carlton Young

FAILURE

"It's everyone's greatest motivation: fear of failure. Everyone I know, anyway. **As you mature, you get more secure, more confident.** But the fear is always there."

Anne Donovan

&

"There's a point to fear. But there's an immobility to it, too. **Fear can make you avoid risk and adventure, and** hide behind a mask of security. Fear can save our lives, but it can also shrivel us up, make us play things safe and **sometimes deny us our greatest joys.**"

Donn Moomaw

I'm a lawyer, b

would like to h

doctor. I was f

medicine, you

college, I convi

I didn't have th

sports and take

courses. No on

couldn't do it —

couldn't do it

t I really
ve been a
...nated by
...ow? But in
...ed myself that
...time to play
re-med
told me I

I told myself

Carlos Álvarez

"Just play the thing out. Play until there's no time left to play."

STATS

- Phi Beta Kappa graduate, Penn State, 1983. Led Penn State to its first national championship with a victory over Georgia in the Sugar Bowl.

- Won Davey O'Brien Award in 1982 as the nation's top quarterback; set 26 Penn State career passing records.

- Drafted by Kansas City Chiefs in the first round of the 1983 NFL draft; played in league for 7 years.

- Currently the lead game analyst for college football at CBS Sports.

- Donated the scholarship from the Davey O'Brien Award to Renaissance Fund, which provides tuition assistance to Penn State students.

When I was a quarterback for the Kansas City Chiefs, where I spent seven years, I sometimes got so frustrated by what I thought *wasn't* happening in my career that I missed out on a lot of the enjoyment of what I *was* doing.

I was an NFL quarterback back when there were only 28 teams. There were only a handful of people in the entire world doing what I was doing! But I didn't appreciate it until I suddenly wasn't playing anymore. That was a huge moment of awakening for me. What I learned from it is that you can't lose sight of the moment. There's nothing wrong with aspiration, with anticipation, looking forward . . . but it's got to be tempered with an appreciation of the here and now. I've tried to live my life ever since with that appreciation.

The main thing I learned from football, though, is the importance of perseverance. A lot of people don't succeed — in football, in other sports, in relationships, in business, in life — for the simplest of reasons: they just don't have a *fourth-quarter mentality*. They don't know how to fight through the times in life when things get tough or disappointing . . . to *play the thing out*.

With this in mind, I witnessed a game when I was in junior high school that made an incredible impact on me. My dad was coaching at the University of Kentucky. This was his first year at Kentucky, and we were playing Alabama at home. Of course, we hadn't beaten them for many years. Kentucky had never been a real powerful football program, certainly not compared to Alabama. But miraculously, we were winning 14-0 at halftime. Everybody was all fired up and we were feeling great. In the third quarter, we were still playing well, although we were starting to get tired. And as the third quarter ended, we were tied 14-14.

Then something strange happened. As the third-quarter clock ran out, we watched the Alabama players stand together, without saying

Todd Blackledge

anything, and they all held up four fingers. This, I was to learn later, was their shorthand way of saying, "Okay, this is the fourth quarter. This is it. The fourth quarter belongs to Alabama. Time to kick in." And kick in they did. They rallied in a big way, when it mattered, and won the game. They played the thing out, to the end, giving it their all until there was no time left to play.

It was devastating and thrilling to watch all at once. But to this day, when I'm faced with a seemingly insurmountable challenge and time is running out, I think to myself, "Four fingers. Four fingers."

Contact Todd Blackledge online at verizonreads.net/lifesplaybook.

COMING FROM BEHIND

"In college I was on a team **that lost only one game in three years.** But you know what? In almost every single one of those games, **we were behind at half time.** Think about it."
JOHN WILSON

perfection

"NO MATTER WHAT YOU ACHIEVE, THERE'S ALWAYS A

NAGGING SENSE OF NOT BEING PERFECT. A LITTLE BIT

OF THAT IS GOOD. BUT YOU CAN'T LET IT TURN INTO

BLIND, DRIVEN AMBITION. YOU'RE JUST SETTING

YOURSELF UP TO BE NEUROTIC." *Michelle Johnson*

"In sports, the gratification is instant. You win or lose, the outcome is clear. In real life, you find out that things aren't quite that cut-and-dried. Not every-thing has the clear results of a sports event."

JACK SIKMA

Time out

You still had baby teeth when you learned how. You've been doing it every day since. And chances are, you fall into one of two groups — those who love it and those who don't. We're talking about reading, of course. But whether you *like* to read is almost as irrelevant as whether you like to breathe — you *need* to read. Here's why:

Education begins with reading.

Reading is one of the first skills kids are taught in school. That's because you must be able to read to keep learning. And the level of education you attain is key in determining the kind of life you'll lead as an adult. On average, a college graduate will earn three times as much as someone without a high school diploma.*

Ask yourself: How has reading helped me acquire a skill or learn about a topic of interest to me?

Reading is the basis for success — no matter how you define it.

People define success in many different ways — a happy family life, a prosperous career, some combination of factors. The relationship between reading and suc-

cess is evident early on — students who read more at home are better readers at school and have higher math scores.**

Ask yourself: In what ways might reading help me achieve the goals I've set for my future?

Reading increases your self-confidence.

The more you know, the better you feel about yourself. Verizon Academic All-America Hall of Famer Jolanda Jones said it best: "People who read well are confident in all aspects of life simply because reading is necessary everywhere."

Ask yourself: In what ways could reading help me overcome obstacles I might encounter in my future?

Reading makes you more interesting!

There's no such thing as "good reading" or "bad reading," so choose topics that interest you. Before you know it, you'll feel at ease talking with anyone — and others will want to hear your thoughts and feelings about all sorts of issues.

Ask yourself: In what ways will reading help me form better relationships with people throughout my life?

* Digest of Education Statistics, 1998
** Educational Testing Service. America's Smallest School: The Family, 1999

Visit Life's Playbook Online for more tips and resources: **verizonreads.net/lifesplaybook**

trying

"I don't have a philosophy of winning — I have a philosophy of *trying*. If you put forth an effort that encompasses your very best — all your intensity, all your enthusiasm — then you can stop worrying about the outcome, because you've done all you can do. By that definition, you're already a winner."

Lee Roy Selmon

"I've always focused on what I have in common with people, rather than why I'm different."

STATS

- A key member of the UCLA basketball dynasty of the 1970s; graduated with a degree in economics, 1974.

- NBA first-round draft pick, won Rookie of the Year honors while helping the Golden State Warriors capture the NBA title in 1975.

- Played on several L.A. Lakers championship squads and was an All-Star.

- Currently a sports/financial business consultant. Donates time and resources to various youth organizations such as the Special Olympics, the Boys and Girls Clubs of America and the March of Dimes Reading Olympics.

Here's a story about ego. When I went from being a star forward at UCLA to the Golden State Warriors — my very first year in the NBA — I was offered a co-starring role in a "blaxploitation" movie. Wow! I asked myself, could I do both? Launch a film career with rookie camp fast approaching? Could I risk co-starring in a feature film and not training for NBA rookie camp, knowing that I'd gone to Golden State as the top rookie pick and they were depending on me? Sure, no problem! In my own mind, I was walking on water. I was invincible.

So I spent two and a half weeks on a film set — under hot lights, sweating, losing all my fluids, getting totally wiped out and dehydrated. And only after that was done did I begin twice-a-day workouts with the Warriors.

Well, I bombed. I couldn't even get through training camp. It was the lowest point of my life.

What did I learn? Well, I learned that you can't let your ego carry you away, in terms of what you think you can do — and that commitments are commitments. I made up my mind there and then to get back into shape, as fast as possible. It made me hungrier than ever to be successful in the NBA. The result? I went on to win the championship, became rookie of the year, and the rest is — sort of — history. But I honestly think that if I hadn't had that early humiliation, that early lesson in the destructive power of ego . . . I wouldn't have had the hunger, the drive, to succeed later on.

As for personal philosophy, I've always felt that, in any situation, whatever the players, if you concentrate on things you have in common with people, rather than why you're different, it's going to go

more smoothly. I get the most out of all relationships — sports, business, personal — by doing that.

I don't mean that you have to agree on everything, or that you even have to like each other. But it creates a positive basis to work on the same team, or on the same project. Even in very sensitive, delicate or awkward situations, focusing on what you have in common somehow makes the disagreements not as disagreeable.

Contact Jamaal Wilkes online at verizonreads.net/lifesplaybook.

SECURITY

"Security comes from earning it — not seeking it."

MARV LEVY

hard work

"IN THE CONTEST BETWEEN TALENT AND HARD WORK AS TO WHICH IS THE MORE IMPORTANT ELEMENT OF SUCCESS, THERE'S NO COMPARISON. A MEDIOCRE TALENT WITH LOTS OF HARD WORK WILL GO MUCH FARTHER THAN A STELLAR TALENT WHO JUST COASTS." *DAVE JOYNER*

ACHIEVE MENT
Achievement
achievement

"One of the daunting things about being an achiever in any field is

that suddenly you have the power to influence people.

Some sports heroes say, 'I don't want that responsibility.' But that's

the wrong reaction. The right reaction is, 'Okay,

I've got some influence. How do I use it to

help someone else be successful too?'" *Tim Foley*

REWARDS

RDS

"STAR ATHLETES AND ACADEMIC ACHIEVERS HAVE TO REALIZE THAT, IN REAL LIFE, NO ONE'S GOING TO BE STANDING BY TO HAND YOU A TROPHY BECAUSE YOU WERE A GOOD FRIEND THAT DAY. THE REWARDS ARE DIFFERENT." MICHELLE JOHNSON

R

e

"A competitive spirit stands anyone in good stead in life. Competition is the way of the world — not negative, cutthroat competition for its own sake, but simply the understanding that no one's going to give you anything for nothing, and that you need to compete to win."

Jack Mildren

STATS

- Won 11 NCAA swimming titles, an all-time record; led Stanford to 3 NCAA team championships.

- At 1984 Olympics (L.A.), won gold in the 400-meter medley relay and silver in the 100-meter butterfly and 200-meter individual medley.

- In 1986, set the world record in the 100-meter butterfly. Elected to the International Swimming Hall of Fame in 1998.

- At Stanford, won J.E. Wallace Sterling Award for community work.

- At 1992 Olympics (Barcelona), won gold in the 100-meter butterfly and in the 400-meter medley relay.

- In 1994, earned a law degree from Cornell, but returned to swimming as assistant men's coach at Stanford for the 1997-98 season, helping Stanford win the 1998 NCAA swimming title.

- Currently head women's swimming coach at San Jose State.

"Sometimes, things don't work out the way you plan

Swimming for me started at age 5, when I began taking swimming lessons with the local Red Cross. Shortly thereafter, my parents enrolled my older sister and me in a formal swim program — I'm sure they thought it would be good for her and figured I would like to tag along. Well since then I've never stopped swimming, and have spent many waterlogged weeks, months and years in the pool throughout the past few decades.

It wasn't until high school that I really made the commitment to swimming. I improved every year — knowing I had an aptitude for the sport and believing I had what it took to be a national competitor, I began setting my sights on competing in the Olympic Games. That, combined with the encouragement I received from my coaches and my peers, helped me keep the focus I needed to go the distance.

Going off to Stanford to experience collegiate swimming for the first time was amazing — it was an environment that helped me

because of factors that are out of your control, or just an off day."

improve tremendously as a swimmer. When I made the '84 Olympic team and won a gold medal in the 400-meter medley relay and silver in two other individual events, it was a dream come true! A lifelong ambition had become reality. I'd been dreaming of the Olympics since the age of 7, after watching Mark Spitz on television — in 1972!

I was able to set a world record and it seemed as though I had reached the height of my career at just the right time — and in Los Angeles in front of the home crowd. What a tremendous experience that was! Then, just as fast as it happened, it all seemed to be over.

Although the Olympic experience had ended I felt that I had more in me — that my best was yet to come. At that point I realized that my swimming career wasn't over and I set my sights on the Seoul Olympics in 1988.

For the next four years I was focused on that objective. I trained harder than I had ever trained before. However, things just didn't

Pablo Morales

seem to click for me in '88. At the Olympic trials at the University of Texas in Austin, my swimming wasn't what it should have been. The U.S. team left for Seoul without me, and I was devastated. I figured my swimming career was over, so with that I packed up and moved on to law school.

As the '92 Olympics began to approach I had the distant idea of possibly coming back to swimming. The dream of making another Olympic team hadn't died inside me. With Barcelona approaching, I decided to pursue swimming again. At that point I had been out of the water for nearly three years and knew many challenges lay ahead — but when I began training, I knew instantly that it was what I wanted to do.

When all was said and done the hard work and dedication paid off. At the age of 27 — old for a swimmer — I won gold in the 100-meter butterfly and in the 400-meter medley relay.

Looking back I can see that not making the '88 team that competed in Seoul led me to develop a certain strength and determination that I might not have had without that disappointment. I also learned that sometimes things in life don't work out the way you plan because of factors that are out of your control, even factors as slight as having an off day. You take from those experiences all that you can and keep working toward your goals — trying to do better next time around.

Contact Pablo Morales online at verizonreads.net/lifesplaybook.

SUCCESS

"I used to want to be successful to please everyone else. True maturity, I think, is **wanting success for yourself.**"
Jolanda Jones

People are human. And humans have problems. Other people can help. Have you given them a chance to try? If you're concerned, confused, worried, frustrated or upset, talk about it. Problems at home, conflicts about grades or job performance, concerns about whether to apply to college or a new job, frustration about juggling too many commitments . . . they all have workable solutions

But no one can do it alone. Share your feelings with someone who can give you honest advice, useful information or just a sympathetic ear. Don't be afraid to talk to:

- Parents or other family members
- Community support groups
- Teachers
- Coaches

- School and career counselors
- Someone at your place of worship
- Psychologists
- Crisis or help hotlines

Visit Life's Playbook Online at **verizonreads.net/ lifesplaybook** for a listing of organizations and other resources you can tap to help with:

- School
- Career
- Sports
- Health
- Family
- Alcohol and drug abuse
- Crisis intervention
- Literacy problems

verizon

Visit Life's Playbook Online for more tips and resources: **verizonreads.net/lifesplaybook**

"Balance

is critical to any student-athlete
trying to master the double burden
of athletics and academics.
In my case, there was no short cut.

*It was just a
matter of discipline."*

OLIVER LUCK

"**Direct contact** between students and teachers is so important. It should be a **collaboration**. I encourage students to befriend teachers, think of them as collaborators, colleagues. **Learn things together**."

SHERWOOD ROWLAND

"It all comes down to the magic word: balance."

STATS

- Graduated from Rice University, 1987; Rhodes Scholar candidate.

- Ranks among the top 6 females in the shot put; a 3-time NCAA outdoor champion and 3-time NCAA indoor champion; earned All-America honors 9 times.

- Named the NCAA Athlete of the Decade for the '80s in women's track and field.

- Earned an M.D. in 1992 from the University of Texas-Houston. Currently a staff child and adolescent psychiatrist at Philhaven Behavioral Healthcare Services in Lebanon, Pa.

- Has volunteered with Harris County (Texas) Children's Mental Health Needs Council; Steering Committee on Youth and Violence Prevention; Special Olympics.

O f all the things I've been blessed with in my life — the miracles that are my children, and my husband Jim — one of the things that I value most is the opportunity to have pursued women's athletics.

As someone who was always on the road to becoming a doctor, I was painfully aware that the academic side of my life would be very demanding — and it always was. But I don't think I would have had nearly as fulfilling a life as I've had without track and field.

I came of age at a time when women's athletics were, perhaps for the first time in history, really being taken very seriously. And as a result, I myself took them seriously.

My dedication to track and field not only got me a scholarship to Rice University — which allowed me to pursue my dream of becoming a physician — but also provided me with friendships, satisfying achievements for the record books, and memories of competitions and competitors that I will cherish all my life.

Today, I work with young people who are mentally challenged — whose lives have been compromised by mental illness. My goal is to help them "get back into their normal lives," as I like to put it. And I often see sports as a wonderful venue to help them do just that.

I'm constantly amazed at the therapeutic effect sports of all kinds have on young people. Recreational sports, competitive sports, any sports — they're all great for improving mental conditioning, building self-confidence, keeping you focused. Sports — and every other extracurricular activity, for that matter — are every bit as important as academics in having a fulfilling life.

It has been my experience that equal dedication to all sides of life — the physical, mental, emotional, social and spiritual — is crucially important. It all comes down to the magic word: balance. It is, in the end, what leads us to excellence, achievement and happiness.

Contact Regina Cavanaugh Murphy online at verizonreads.net/lifesplaybook.

Regina Cavanaugh Murphy

Living in the Present

- Earned 4 letters in track, 3 in football and 1 in basketball at Coe College.

- Graduated Phi Beta Kappa and Magna Cum Laude, Coe College, 1950.

- Retired as head coach of the NFL's Buffalo Bills, which he led to 4 consecutive Super Bowls and 6 AFC East titles.

- Awarded AFC Coach of the Year in 1988 and 1993.

- Spokesman for the Literacy Volunteers of America and United Way Services; honorary board member for the Roswell-Park Cancer Alliance.

"Football doesn't build character. It *reveals* character."

Having been a coach in the NFL, I'm approached all the time by people asking, "So how do you get to be a coach in the NFL?" It really frosts me! It also makes me realize the mistake so many people make of not living in the present. Goals are great, but if you live in constant anticipation of something else, of *getting* somewhere, you're never fully involved in what you're doing now. And I think that means you're probably not doing a great job.

I entered coaching because I loved it — *wherever* I was. And believe me, I've been all over — Canada, California, Virginia, Buffalo, Montreal, Washington. But wherever I was, *that* was my dream job. I even loved coaching high school. My philosophy is that, whatever your job, do it as though you're going to be doing it for the rest of your life. Because once you start to see it as a stepping stone to something else, you're not doing your best; you're not fully involved.

What's the secret of coaching? It's being a good teacher. Sure, styles of coaching may differ — you can be bombastic like Vince Lombardi, or soft-spoken like Bud Wilkinson, or a "master of the fundamentals" like John Wooden, who emphasized a philosophical approach. But at the end of the day, a coach is a teacher.

One bromide I've always disagreed with is that sports — say, football — can build character. I don't think any sport builds character. A sport *reveals* character. It takes a lot more than a game to shape someone's character — but a game provides an environment in which the good qualities in a person's character can respond. One of the most important qualities: the ability to be heroic in defeat.

Contact Marv Levy online at verizonreads.net/lifesplaybook.

Marv Levy

Life's Playbook For Success
End *Zone*

The Verizon Academic All-America® Team members: Who are they?

The Verizon Academic All-America Team members are students who have found that critical balance between drive and relaxation. Between work and play. Between school and sports (or other activities). Between going for it now . . . and preparing for later.

They are college student-athletes from around the U.S. who are recognized each year for achievements both on the playing field and in the classroom. They have managed to be successful — in some cases despite tough odds and many obstacles.

The Teams Program: How does it work?

The Academic All-America Teams Program was created in 1952 by CoSIDA, the College Sports Information Directors of America, to honor the athletes who excel not just in sports, but also in academics. Under an agreement with CoSIDA, Verizon has been the exclusive sponsor of the Verizon Academic All-America Teams Program since 1985. The role of academics in a college athlete's life has become one of the most important issues in college sports today. The Verizon Academic All-America Teams Program rewards individuals who have excelled in two very difficult and challenging areas: the classroom and the playing field. No other award acknowledges as many student-athletes for the hard work, success and balance they achieve in sports and academics.

The Verizon Academic All-America Teams Program annually names and honors almost 700 student-athletes to five men's teams (football, basketball, baseball, fall/winter at-large and spring at-large) and five women's teams (volleyball, basketball, softball, fall/winter at-large and spring at-large) in two divisions — University Division (Division IA-IAA) and College (NCAA Divisions II-III and NAIA). Athletes from all sports in which the NCAA conducts championships are eligible. A key objective of the program is to position these student-athletes as role models for today's youth.

Each year, numerous Verizon Academic All-America Team members have been members of national championship teams. Many others have been named national players of the year in their sports and have been winners of other prestigious national awards.

For a searchable listing of Team members, visit Life's Playbook Online at **verizonreads.net/lifesplaybook**.

What is CoSIDA?

The College Sports Information Directors of America (CoSIDA) is an association that represents over 1,800 professionals who serve as the sports public relations directors for universities and colleges in the United States and Canada. CoSIDA began selecting Academic All-America Teams in 1952 with a University Division football team and has continually expanded since, adding men's basketball and baseball in the 1960s, a college division for all existing teams in the 1970s, and women's basketball in 1979. Volleyball, softball and the at-large teams were added in the early '80s and a fall/winter at-large team was added in 1995 to supplement the existing spring at-large teams.

What is the Hall of Fame?

In 1988, Verizon and CoSIDA decided to extend the Verizon Academic All-America Teams Program to honor former Team members who have made outstanding accomplishments in their professions and substantial contributions to their communities. The Verizon Academic All-America Hall of Fame was then created to honor these individuals. The first year's Hall of Famers were inducted in 1988, with between four and six individuals inducted each year since. Currently, there are 63 individuals in the Verizon Academic All-America Hall of Fame.

What is Verizon?

Verizon Communications is one of the world's leading providers of communications services. Verizon companies are the largest providers of wireline and wireless communications in the United States, with 95 million access lines and 25 million wireless customers. A Fortune 10 company with more than 260,000 employees and approximately $60 billion in 1999 revenues, Verizon's global presence extends to 40 countries in the Americas, Europe, Asia and the Pacific. For more information on Verizon, visit **verizon.com**.

ROSTER OF HALL OF FAME INDUCTEES

Val Ackerman
University of Virginia, '81
Basketball/Political and
Social Thought
Today: President, WNBA
HOF Induction: 1999

Danny Ainge
Brigham Young Univ., '92
Basketball/Communications
Today: TV Basketball Analyst
HOF Induction: 2000

Carlos Alvarez
Florida, '72
Football/Political Science
Today: Environmental and
Land Use Lawyer
HOF Induction: 1989

Alan Ameche
Wisconsin, '55
Football/Communication Arts
HOF Induction: 1992
(Deceased)

Terry Baker
Oregon State, '63
Football/Mechanical
Engineering
Today: Lawyer
HOF Induction: 1991

Raymond Berry
SMU, '55
Football/Business
Administration
Today: Retired NFL Coach
HOF Induction: 1993

Todd Blackledge
Penn State, '83
Football/Speech
Communications
Today: TV College
Football Analyst
HOF Induction: 1997

Willie Bogan
Dartmouth, '71
Football/Spanish
Today: Corporate Attorney
HOF Induction: 1989

Bill Bradley
Princeton, '65
Basketball/History
Today: Former U.S. Senator
HOF Induction: 1988

Steven Bramwell
Washington, '67
Football/Pre-Medicine
Today: Orthopedic Surgeon
HOF Induction: 1989

Dave Casper
Notre Dame, '74
Football/Economics
Today: Insurance
District Agent
HOF Induction: 1993

Regina Cavanaugh Murphy
Rice University, '87
Track and Field/Human
Physiology
Today: Child Psychiatrist
HOF Induction: 2000

Doug Collins
Illinois State, '81
Basketball/Physical
Education
Today: TV Basketball
Analyst
HOF Induction: 1995

Leigh Curl
Connecticut, '85
Basketball/Biology
Today: Assistant Professor
of Orthopedic Surgery,
Univ. of Maryland
HOF Induction: 1998

Pete Dawkins
Army, '59
Football
Today: Vice Chairman and
Executive Vice President,
Citigroup
HOF Induction: 1988

Anne Donovan
Old Dominion, '83
Basketball/Recreational
Services
Today: Head Coach,
WNBA's Charlotte Sting
HOF Induction: 1994

Stephen Eisenhauer
Navy, '54
Football/Engineering
Today: Flight Consultant
and Technical Advisor
HOF Induction: 1992

Bob Elliott
Arizona, '77
Basketball/Business
Administration
Today: Accountant and
Basketball Analyst
HOF Induction: 1995

Dick Enberg
Honorary Inductee
Central Michigan
University, '57
Baseball/Health Science
Today: Sports Broadcaster,
Spokesperson for Verizon
Academic All-America
Teams Program
HOF Induction: 1997

Tim Foley
Purdue, '70
Football/Industrial
Economics
Today: Marketing Company
President
HOF Induction: 1997

John Fowler
UCLA, '78
Football/Biochemistry
Today: Assistant Professor,
Dokuz Eylul University
(Izmir, Turkey)
HOF Induction: 1999

Jim Grabowski
Illinois, '66
Football/Finance
Today: Consultant
HOF Induction: 1993

Randy Gradishar
Ohio State, '74
Football/Education
Today: President, Denver
Broncos Youth Foundation
HOF Induction: 1992

Pat Haden
USC, '75
Football/English
Today: Attorney,
Football Analyst
HOF Induction: 1988

Chad Hennings
Air Force, '88
Football/Management
Today: Retired from NFL,
Dallas Cowboys
HOF Induction: 1999

**Jeannie Demers
Henningsen**
Buena Vista University, '87
Basketball/Elementary
Education
Today: Third-Grade Teacher
HOF Induction: 1999

Joe Holland
Cornell, '78
Football/History and English
Today: Attorney
HOF Induction: 1991

Michelle Johnson
Air Force, '81
Basketball/Political Science
and Economics
Today: U.S. Air Force Colonel
HOF Induction: 1995

Jolanda Jones
University of Houston, '89
Track & Field,
Heptathlon/Political Science
Today: Attorney
HOF Induction: 1999

Lester Jordan
Honorary Inductee
SMU
Founder, AAA Program
HOF Induction: 1990
(Deceased)

David Joyner
Penn State, '72
Football/Pre-Medicine
Today: Orthopedic Surgeon
HOF Induction: 1991

Bernie Kosar
Miami, '85
Football/Finance
and Economics
Today: Corporate Senior
Advisor
HOF Induction: 1998

Marv Levy
Honorary Inductee
Coe College, '50
Football/Economics
and Pre-Law
Today: Retired NFL Coach
HOF Induction: 1998

Oliver Luck
West Virginia University, '82
Football/History
Today: Founder and President
of The Luck Group
HOF Induction: 2000

Ellen Mayer-Sabik
Cornell, '84
Gymnastics/Pre-Medicine
Today: Cardiologist
HOF Induction: 1997

Pablo Morales
Stanford, '87
Swimming/English
Today: Head Women's Swim-
ming Coach, San Jose State
HOF Induction: 2000

J. Richard "Rich" Mayo
Air Force, '61
Football/Engineering
Today: Specialist in
Addiction Medicine
HOF Induction: 1994

Merlin Olsen
Utah State, '62
Football/Business
Today: Professional Actor
and Spokesperson
HOF Induction: 1988

Tom McMillen
Maryland, '74
Basketball/Chemistry
Today: Chairman and CEO,
Complete Wellness
Centers, Inc.
HOF Induction: 1988

Ron Perry
Holy Cross, '80
Basketball/Economics
Today: Real Estate Executive
HOF Induction: 1996

Jack Mildren
Oklahoma, '72
Football/Petroleum Land
Management
Today: Investor/Businessman
HOF Induction: 1998

Pat Richter
Wisconsin, '64
Football/Landscape
Architecture
Today: Athletic Director,
University of Wisconsin
HOF Induction: 1995

Wade Mitchell
Georgia Tech, '57
Football/Textiles
Today: Retired Bank
Executive
HOF Induction: 1996

Sherwood Rowland
Honorary Inductee
Ohio Wesleyan University, '48
Basketball and Baseball/
Chemistry
Today: Nobel Laureate;
Professor, University of
California, Irvine
HOF Induction: 2000

Donn Moomaw
UCLA, '54
Football/Physical Education
Today: Retired Minister,
Bel Air Presbyterian Church
HOF Induction: 1988

Joe Romig
Colorado, '63
Football/Physics
Today: Physicist and Consul-
tant on Fires and Explosions
HOF Induction: 1989

Lee Roy Selmon
Oklahoma, '75
Football/Special Education
Today: Associate Athletic
Director, University of
South Florida
HOF Induction: 1994

Jack Sikma
Illinois Wesleyan, '76
Basketball/Accounting
Today: President of Golf
Course/Restaurant
Development Company
HOF Induction: 1998

Tracy Caulkins Stockwell
Florida, '85
Swimming/
Telecommunications
Today: Assists Australia's
Olympic Committee
HOF Induction: 1997

Brock Strom
Air Force, '59
Football/Engineering Science
Today: Retired Air
Force Colonel
HOF Induction: 1991

Jim Swink
Texas Christian, '57
Football/Pre-Medicine
Today: Orthopedic Surgeon
HOF Induction: 1989

Steve Taylor
Delaware, '80
Baseball/Education
Today: Insurance Sales
Executive
HOF Induction: 1990

Joe Theismann
Notre Dame, '71
Football/Sociology
Today: TV Football Analyst
HOF Induction: 1990

Bob Thomas
Notre Dame, '74
Football/Government
Today: Justice, Illinois
Supreme Court Second
District
HOF Induction: 1996

Howard Twilley
Tulsa, '68
Football/Electrical
Engineering
Today: Financial Consultant,
Merrill Lynch
HOF Induction: 1990

Bill Walton
UCLA, '74
Basketball/History
Today: TV Sports
Broadcaster
HOF Induction: 1994

Kermit Washington
American, '73
Basketball/Psychology
Today: Restaurant Owner
HOF Induction: 1993

Lynette Woodard
Kansas, '81
Basketball/Communications
Today: Formerly with the
WNBA's Detroit Shock
HOF Induction: 1992

Justice Byron White
Honorary Inductee
Colorado, '38
Football/Economics
Today: Retired U.S.
Supreme Court Justice
HOF Induction: 1996

John Wooden
Honorary Inductee
Purdue, '32
Basketball/Physical
Education
Today: Author, Retired
NCAA Basketball Coach
HOF Induction: 1994

Jamaal Wilkes
UCLA, '74
Basketball/Economics
Today: Sports/Financial
Business Consultant
HOF Induction: 1990

Carlton Young
Villanova, '83
Track/Biology
Today: Pancreas Transplant
Surgeon
HOF Induction: 1996

John Wilson
Michigan State, '53
Football/History
Today: Retired President,
Washington and
Lee University
HOF Induction: 1989

Learn more about all of the Verizon Academic All-America® Hall of Famers
at Life's Playbook Online: **verizonreads.net/lifesplaybook**.

Index of Quotes

Hall of Famer	Quote Topic / Page Number
Val Ackerman	Role Models (82)
Carlos Alvarez	Limiting Yourself (108)
Raymond Berry	Focus (20)
Todd Blackledge	Persistence (80)
Dave Casper	Happiness (93)
Regina Cavanaugh Murphy	Reading (60)
Anne Donovan	Fear and Failure (107), Role Models (89)
Bob Elliott	Recognizing Authority (87), Rules (103)
Tim Foley	Achievement (122), Role Models (16)
John Fowler	Learning from Sports (39)
Chad Hennings	Teamwork (21)
Jeannie Demers Henningsen	Role Models (83)
Joe Holland	Reading (60)
Michelle Johnson	Advice (52), Perfection (113), Rewards (123), Self-Doubt (15)
Jolanda Jones	Reading (66, 72), Success (128)
Dave Joyner	Hard Work (121), Role Models (88)
Bernie Kosar	Academics (50)
Marv Levy	Character (101), Security (120)
Oliver Luck	Balance (130), Reading (92)
Rich Mayo	Role Models (88)
Tom McMillen	Reaching Goals (32)
Jack Mildren	Advice (52), No Excuses (65), Competition (124)
Donn Moomaw	Fear and Failure (107), Mistakes (85)
Merlin Olsen	Perseverance (33)
Ron Perry	Standing Out (71)
Pat Richter	Academics (50)
Sherwood Rowland	Learning (131)
Lee Roy Selmon	Trying (116), Winning (34)
Jack Sikma	Learning from Sports (114), Self-Esteem (14)
Brock Strom	Advice (52)
Steve Taylor	Fear (59)
Bob Thomas	The Role of Sports (94)
Bill Walton	Teamwork (77)
Kermit Washington	Insecurity (45)
John Wilson	Coming from Behind (112), Role Models (16)
John Wooden	Accomplishment (58)
Carlton Young	Ambition (24), Control (76), Failure (106), Sports (49)

ACKNOWLEDGMENTS

Sincere thanks to the many members of the Verizon Academic All-America Hall of Fame who contributed their time and valuable insights to this project. Without their help and enthusiasm this book would not have been possible.

CREDITS

Project Management: J.D. Morgan Associates

Creative & Production Management: Media Management Services, Inc.

Writing: Mark Gauthier

Research & Photo Archives: Millsport, Inc.

Design: Acme, A Marketing and Design Company

Illustration: Gary Alphonso, Kyle Dreier

Cover Photo and Principal Portrait Photography: Bill Cramer

Photo, p. 101: John Huet, from the book "Soul of the Game" (Melcher/Workman)

Photo, p. 127: Tim Davis